HOW TECHNOLOGY MARKET DEVELOPMENT

TO DEVELOPING COUNTRIES

JOHN LOK

ISBN 979-888591023-1

Contents

Preface

This book explains what factors can be sudden to influence some countries people feel high technological products demand. I shall indicate Afica is one developing country, how cultural improvement factor can influence many African feel more needs to buy different kinds of high technological products to use to satisfy their living needs. This book uses a descriptive methodology of system analysis to explain whether technology is needed on economic progress or not, and whether technological innovation can raise efficiency and more productivity to all industries or not, even encourages consumer behaviors. The only solution for raising productivity and efficiency, who are losing out in the race is investment in all its forms, in both equipment and people. This analysis will be of interest to all those faced with economic decisions: engineers, managers, scientists and administrators as well as economists need to learn how to use technology to solve low efficiency and low productivity challenges. When any industries can apply technology to raise productivities, whether it will increase to supply any products to satisfy consumer demand as well as improve marketing development to any customers when they can attempt to sell any kinds of products to use in any time. So, I feel that technological innovation can bring direct positive relationsip to encourage consumer buying behaviours easily.

This is a book for economists by training who doubt the current efficacy of the solutions which whose discipline traditionally prescribes, as economic dominance begins to move with the technology to parts of the world that only a short time ago were considered " less developed". This book presents an analysis of economic processes which does not require hypotheses. It shows how economies evolve through the deliberate action not only of individual, but also of firm, governments and business organizations and students who have interest to judge whether the technological innovation will be one production of factor to any organizations or or how the technologial innovation can brought what kinds of external or internal factors to influence to the organization after whose organization changed to technological innovation of organizational structure.

Is technological innovation into the industrial base of new products or processes, including modifications to existing process equipment which significantly reduce its cost of operation? The physical difference between industrialised countries and the developed high technological countries is the technological hardware, i.e. the factories, distribution systems and all the fixed capital investment which have accumulated. technological innovation is really effort to influence our economic development nowadays. Finally, whether technological innovation can excite consumer buying desires absolutely. I shall on technological innovation, internet innovation these two production of factors aspects to explain how andh wy they can excite consumer needs.

I hope any high technological products businessmen can know how to let the less number of high technological products need buyers to change their high technological products need to be raised. So, when high technological product businessmen can understand what factors can raise the country people feel high technological products needs , then they can attempt to achieve the important factors to cause their high technological products demand increases in possible.

Prologue

CHAPTER ONE

Technological innovation factor excites consumer buying need

● How technological innovation factor
excites consumer buying

When one country owns more industries can apply high technological manufacturing method to raise productive products. When they can apply high technology to increase to manufacture any products number (increasing supply). So, it won't bring shortage to supply any products to satisfy consumers' demand when their products can be accepted to choose to buy in preference in consumer market. It will bring real bulk of products supply benefits to saitisfy unlimited customer demand to the kind of product. So, it seems that high technological innovation method can achieve the enough product supply number to satisfy global consumers' buying needs. For example, smart phones products are needed high technological manufacturing method to produce . If smart phones can be applied high technological manufacturing machines to raise their supply number. Then, global smart phone consumers will buy any kinds of smart phones from smarts phone shops in any time easily. So, it can satisfy smart phone consumers' real time purchase needs in any time. It can can solve shortage of smart phones supply to any countries consumers as well as they have many different kinds of smart phones products to choose to buy any time.

I shall explain how one technological innovative manufacturing method, for example robotic factory manufacturing environment as below:

Robotic manufacturing system may be physical , like the solar system or an ecological system or which may be simply behavioral, like an organization. For example, a national economy may be a system, markets are systems, firms and factories are systems. Even, families and individuals are economic systems. The economy of the largest systems, national economy, may be called macroeconomy, which deals in terms of national aggregates for output, income, productivity. The economics of small systems, which are their parts or subsystems may be called microeconomics.

A robotic manufaturing system transforms inputs into outputs. An economic system is such a process. For example, robotic manufacturing factories are as systems take in raw materials, services etc. and change them into products for sale, i.e. output and consume them, thereby transforming them into rubbish, incidential is bad output. Also, countries consume their actural resources to enhance their standard of living and change them into waste products. If the system in question is national economy, some of the subsystems are might consider to be: the government, the firms, the consumers, the natural resources which it has at its disposal. Each subsystem is itself composed of subsystem of a lower order, such as a firm and each of these can be decomposed into further subsystems, depending on the purpose of the analysis. " All subsystems" interact need have individual characteistics, i.e. they are synergistic if they expected to raise producivity or efficiency or effectively. So, it needs high technological assistance to raise whose ability in economic view.

However, an economic system must continually adapt and restructure to meet the challenges of a changing economic environment if it is to prosper. For example, a firm must respond to its environment in the form of it customers' needs threats from its competitors, government regulations etc. Nowadays, technological innovation process and the nature of social economic and social changes which is occurring as the same time. So, organizations need to have strategic management to raise technological innovation to achieve raising productivity and efficiency aim in order to satisfy global consumers' real time unlimited needs, e.g. different kinds of smart phones sale number.

   ● Can technological innovation factor
achieve the real consumer short time need desire

What is economic process? It consists of the production and consumption of products and services by human. It is a process devised by human for own benefit pupose only. In the past, human lack advanced technological invention, e.g. family society required a much greater degree of organizational skill than hunting and gathering, it seems farming society does not need to achieve efficiency or productivity aim, because it is not industralized manufacturing society. Nowadays, the investment of resourcs is required for manufacturing processes for robotic manufacturing factories. The (AI)manufacturing stage thus needs machines, but it extends the economic process into the processing of manufacturing things, such as food. So, the knowledge and skills to do this are much more specialized again than farmer's or hunter's. So, technological innovation is needed to raise efficient productivity in factories, e.g. the increasing skills of manufacturing and the use of more intensive energy resources, such as coal and oil, gas, even solar energy either resources are from the sun or resources are from earth, e.g. fuels , heat, light, sound utilitiesm liquids , gases,solids. So, technological innovation is important to influence our economic development in our societies, because it can satisfy unlimited consumers needs in any time, such as applying robotic manufacturing method produces different kinds of smart phones products to let global smart phones consumers can choose which style of smart phone is the most suitable style to buy in smart phone shops any time. Then, when the smart phone shop can have enough different kinds of smarts phones to let any visitors to choose to buy. Consequently, when they can compare which price is the most reasonable and which function is the best from different kinds of smart phones choices in the shop. Their success of purchase of any kinds of smart phones chance must increase, when the smart phone shop has enough different kinds of smart phones to let them to choose to buy in any real time in the shop.

Economists usually classify what who call future of production into land, labor and capital. Why technological innovation is one another factor of production. For example, the economic process indicates that the first step is resources from the earth, e.g. solar energy supplies to earth to satisfy human needs. In the economic process, it needs these both supplies, driving force of transformation energy supply and captalyst , such as skills, knowledge, organization, creativity, creative participation in consumptions supply. Then, manufacturers shall change these both supplies to production and distribution of ordered materials and utilities in the economic process. Finally, it will provide to human consumption and human spent resources returned to earth in the final step. Another example of the elements of the economic process: the input is driving force of transformation stage of energy sources, e.g. sunlight firewood, oil and gas, coal , nuclear and household and industrial waste. Next is the economic process stage: facilitators, it includes tangible facilitator includes skills, knowledge, organization, creativity, e.g. language, science, technology, industry, machine, politics, law and order, defence, strategic plan, information systems, administration, tangible facilitator includes incentive system, e.g. money, banking, insurance, shares, private or public organizations, markets, land area. Finally, is the product of innovation stage, it includes utilities , such as electricity , heat, light, sound, motive power as well as ordered materials (products) , such as bread, meat, mine, shoes, clothes, houses, television, roads (public goods) etc.

● How innovation information factor influences the product successful sale

What is the role of innovation information? Any markets requires product or service suppliers rationally act on the basic such information. But what who can't know in advance is how all the other participants are going to behave. The market clearing price would already be known. There would in fact be agreed prices and which everything could be exchanged, and there would be no market system at all. And so who come to market to settle the price/quantity relationship. The theory is that which will arrive at a single price and quantity which reflect supply and demand. However, the number of interactions or pieces of information to be transmitted doubles with every new participants. However, the requirement for information is not limited to the particular market in question. A compromise between the number of people needed to make more nearly " perfect" in the economic sense, and the quantity of information needed to allow it to arrive at a unique price/quantity relationship. The concept of degrees of freedom is widely used in different technological forms, e.g. engineering industry, the equipment is used by manufacturers to make pencils will be worn out to some extent in the process, and this forms an energy path straight to earth from the market in which the equipment was bought. Similarly wear and tear on the equipment used to make the intermediates and the raw materials will also form direct paths to earth from the markets in which were bought. It seems technological innovation factor of production can bring the pencil stationery product innovation when the new pencil stationey product is produced the more excellent quality by the new machines innovation. So, the technological innovation can change the traditional pencil stationery product to become the new machine pencil stationery product to excite schools or offices to use when they need to produce many pencils to use ,e.g. 100 number in short time. This new kind of new machine of pencil stationery product can replace the traditional hand pencil stationery product because anyone does not need to spend much time to increase pencil number to use, they can use pencil stationery machine to produce many pencils to use in short time. This is one kind of new technological of pencil stationery machine product when manufacturing technological is innovated to invent this kind of new machine of pencil stationery writing product.

In an economic system which is working " perfectly" according to the definitations, output is therefore a function of available energy and the technological skills to apply it to conversion of inputs into materials and utilities . In a market economy, given the availability of inputs of energy and materials, and the necessary information, the only factor which can bring this about in the long term is a change in the energy efficiency of its conversion process, i.e. the energy consumed unit of output of the same total production. This depends in the application of skills and design, that is technology factor of production.

Why does innovative information can influence product sale ability? For example, the commodity is technologically complex like a computer, an aircraft or even a refrigetator. One is buying not just the piece of equipment, but also its specification because few people would understand the parts of the machine, let alone be able to judge their quality. Furthermore, one is also buying the future performance of the machine in operationm , its fuel consumptionm reliability, service costs, length of life, resistance to obsolescence etc. Probably the only guarantee that any information obtained on these points is valid is the reputation of the manufacturer. Purchasers estimate chose chances of surviving the guarante period. Brand names are a way of simplisfying information flows. Such problems of defining the commodity and so handling the information necessary to arrive at a stable price, are magnified when counterfeit products, such as are flooding on to the market at present, find their way into markets for genuine products. Buyers will be unable to distinguish unless who are experts and sometimes that may need chemical analysis or destructive testing. This is a recent phenomenon to buy technological products.

● Technological manufacturing innovation production factor brings time information benefit
to excite consumer buying desire

The factory manufacturing system in the real world includes as below:

The first is manual work (manpower) element, in effect the provision of an elementary utility for consumption in a conversion process. If labors are not providing manpower, who become unemployed. Unemployment is not simply leaving a resource at a particular time, it is an injustice and a burden one the very real society which economics is supposed to help. Moreover, the unemployed can't spend the money who don't earn, and so buyers are reward from the economic process.

The second is catalytic skills, knowledge, organization and creativity element which applied to the conversion processes which turn raw materials into products and utilities for consumption. In this case, who are as varied as the individuals that make up mankind, their accumulated knowledge, their capability of organising themselves to achieve their ends and not least their creativity,the ability to generate entirely new catalytic effects.

Finally, is the incentive element, which is the prospect of participating in comsumption of the products of the economic process. The incentive system is cash for current or future exchange for products and utilities. The incentive system must be within the control of the social system of which it is a part. It can only be addressed by society as the whole system. However, for the individual and the firm too the creative must by definition come from outside and it is also depend on the rest of society.

What kinds of product can link between markets. However, there are products which are linked in a different way by associated use. For products anyone who buys a vehicle must also be prepared to buy its fuel, tyres etc. A decision to buy the vehicle therefore automatically generates subsequent expenditure in the other markets. These markets are not so much competitors for buyers' money as complementary to each other. Sale in one must lead to sales in the other. This technological products have the same point, it is that which are needed to attempt to innovate their quality to raise their competitive ability to win their competitors. It seems that technological innovation can be a factor production to these different brands of vehicles and which related link products. Much the same occurs in technological industry. A company may feel that it is wise to buy related pieces of equipment from the same manufacturer, especially if they have to be connected in some way, whatever the price, within reason.

The analysis has shown that two sorts of information are essential of the market is to reach " equilibrium" values of price and quantity: information concerns on the economic environment, which participants can obtain before the market opens; and information about the process of bargaining displayed, which can only be made available as the bargaining proceeds. However, buyers and sellers happen next. If the information acts as a reference point, it can only be a historical one. This is particularly so where markets operate continuously. There is always a lapse between the conclusion of deals and their display, so that new deals are always influenced to be not update information , in the absence of the most recent data, if dealing is busy. So, timing of information ought to be kept the most update to let buyers can have more confidence to make final choice to buy the broad of products. The quality of information which had to passed during bargaining in order to achieve on a unique price/quantity relationship increased rapidly with the number of participants because of the need of to allow everyone of buyers to interact with all the others.

It follows therefore, that as the number of participants becomes very large, the necessary information flows become much larger still and the time needed to allow this to take place increases greatly. So, timing of information can influence the participants would have changed or would have not changed their minds or gone home before proceedings could draw to a close. So, price and quality is the main message of information to influence consume individual attitude to decide to buy the product in market.

Timing of information can influence business cycles. It is well known that business activity is cyclinal. The short cycles of 4 to 5 years are best established , but consumers believe who can discern longer term and even very long term cycles of activity with periods of up to 50 years. Cyclical behavior, can only occur where these is an imperfect response to change, because of imperfect information. In general, this sort could not caused by the response time behavior of individual markets. Whatever the nature of the link, it is clearly the case that the price/quality relationship in individual markets is varying independently of the factors which might normally be expected to affect it in isolated systems. So, cyclical phenomena in business are strong evidence of the market process network behaving as a system.

In conclusion, markets are activites to exchange products and services. The elements of economic chains together to allow modern industrial economies or technological economy to function with all their complexity. They are essential to change and they permit innovation. However, markets are not well represented by the conventional supply/demand schedules, in particular because these can not include the effects of time as an variable factor. It is much clear to represent timing of information as systems in the form of flow diagrams showing the movement of products from innovative processes through markets to consume. Revenue from the market then supplies feedback to product manufacturers, and the whole system responds at different rates to different levels of feedback from clients. An effective medium of exchange is necessary for proper responses to be made.

The complexity of the modern world, where price and quantity and quality in the market are all can't exist without the timing of information factor influence. Price signals are often confused by products, imperfect or incomprehensible information and the various effects of time, and in any case quantities to be supplied to the market have to be decided well in advance of market day.

The whole trend a modern industrial economy or technological economy is towards product differentiation. Such as mobile phone, laptop computer etc. technologic products. Manufacturers often need to innovate design, quality, functions to adapt to client's individual need. So, technological innovation is often a production of factors to invent high technological products. Services too can't be fitted into price/quantity schedules because it is impossible to define the product. Otherwise, the categorisation of human as labor, having a price/quantity relationship, when who are clearly , each is an individual learning system, changing every day of whose life and changing the economic process accordingly. In fact, human must necessarily be accepted as a feature of modern life, to protect to let them to enjoy high quality of life. So, individual economic stage will be needed to enter technological economic stage in consumers' unlimited products choice consumption environment. Indeed by limiting the rate of change such actions may in no small measure be a condition of stability for the people in an economy . It seems that technological innovation is one factor of production and it has close relstionship to timing of reasonable price and quality information to persuade consumers to choose to buy the manufacturer's product.

● TECHNOLOGICAL INNOVATIVE MANUFACTURING BENEFIT TO FACTORY
AND SELLER

On the increasing product supply choice hand, in conversion processes there is always some wear and tear of the fixed asset, the equipment, building etc. which reduce their capacity to produce in future. Of course after the money has been spent on the plant, it is no longer cost of operating. This is not technological obsolescence which results from development of better ways of meeting market needs. The efficiency of produrers is continually improved and the most effective use of the resources available is continually improved and the most effective use of the resources available to the society, and the most effective use of the resources available to the society is made according to the criteria of economic values. The under-utilised resources locked up in the inefficient operation are not necessarily lost. The producer may learn in time to use them better. So that who can eventually compete on moral equal terms, or who may give way to another who knows how to manage the resources more efficiently. If however, the inefficiency has a deep-rooted cause which can not be remedied, or even a producer who is capable of improvement but refuses to act, then the resources run down to extiaction faster than ordinary wear and tear would cause them to. So, it suppose to technological innovation can help producers to reduce cost for long term. It is cost benefit to producers for long term.

For agricultural industry example, it was said that the only way for a farmer to increase whose not revenue significantly, once who was farming as efficiently as possible, was to increase the area of land under cultivation. But technological innovation is such production of factor, it might be a case for increasing the area under cultivation in order to make better use of a piece of equipment, such as a tractor, and so spread its cost over more production. Another might be in the processing industries, such as petrochemicals or oil where many new producers with the same global threats and opportunities. The input costs when products or utilities move in the direction of time and energy in the economic process. If one opportunity for using the resources is selected, then another potential use will be foregone. Opportunity costs are therefore distinguished from input costs by time. So, the production for factor of technological innovation can be opportunity cost, if the manufacturer felt who can spend less manufacturing expenditure for long term. Due to who lose to use money to spend other expenditure or invest, who choose to invent technological innovation to reduce long term input costs. The best opportunities are those which maximise prices and minimise costs.

Producers try to achieve higher market prices by giving their products some distinguishing feature which whose hope will attract buyers away from other competitors and /or generate new buyers, what marketers call product differentiation. In effect they try to move their product into a new market, perhaps thought of as " up market" or a " market niche", but certainly in separate market for analytical purpose. Even if they can not do this, which is unusual in these days of increasing technological innovation and communication , operators continually try to improve their processes in order to reduce costs. If always requires the investment of new resources, e.g. technological innovation.

In the real world, it is not possible to differentiate products or processes except in time. Such as smart phone cause, when one factory can apply robotic manufacturing technology to assist or replace workers to manufacture different kinds of smart phones in bulk in the same time. Then, it will provide many different kinds of smart phones to let smart phones consumers to choose to buy, e.g. the shop can increase from only 10 kinds to 50 kinds of different design of smart phones products to let smart phones consumers to choose when they visit any one shop. Then, every shop's smart phone sale chance must raise when they have 50 kinds of smart phones design to let anyone to choose in any one shop any time. The overall result is to move the process in the direction of economic improvements, in effect the behavior of economic system as a learning system. Time introduces all the risks and opportunities which present themselves to the processor. In the analysis which follows , we classify and illustrate the various aspects of economy of scope under the traditional economic heading of labor, capital, and land. Energy and information, technological innovation are considered too ,because which are fundamental to all systems and process in economic activity and excite consumer purchase desire more easily.

On the division of labor benefits hand. This is a complex process into stages in which a worker can specialize, thus allowing who to perform that particular task more efficiently, i.e. at lower cost per unit of effective output than if who had to undertake the whole process. Such an improvement in efficiency results from the more effective learning, greater development of skills and more intensive application over a period of time which becomes possible when a task is easily within the capacity of one person.

It is easily confused with advances in technology, capital investment or scale of operation. Division of complex process into stages may subsequently allow the development of specialised technologies for the individual stages, and this may result in specialised equipment, and hence capital investment . Similiarly, if the process is carried out with less labor and/or lower raw material costs for each unit of output, those concerned may in principle decide either the produce more . Output or the produce the same output with less input. It seems technological innovation can bring low cost benefits. In fact, new technology imposes a diseconomy on the old, eg. functions using old technology are at a cost disadvantage and must adopt or eventually disappear under free competition. So, new technology is the source of growth and adoptation in economy. The solutions to a diseconomy of scape lies in a change of scope, for example, in this case different establishments operating at different times, and perhaps with different prices. If capital investment are differentiated be improved to give longer life and better use, which in effect reduces their cost in use. For example, continuing advantages in technology allow processes to be designed in such a way that which deliver the same output with ever decreasing inputs of materials, labor or energy. Thus waste is minimised by planning and the conservation of process energy, and maintenance is reduced by change of design or the use of new materials. It may often worth spending more on equipment initially to reduce those time dependent costs. This sort of efficiency is the most obvious effect of scope rather than scale.

Deterioration and obsolescence means wear and tear are the changes which occur in artefacts as which are used , i.e. deterioration , or changes in quality or scope with time. These are not simply time effects because which depend both on the original design and on the conditions of use, such as maintenance skills and even simple care and attention. Obsolescence is difference to depreciation, it relates to the battle in the market place . The networks of markets brings products and therefore all conversion processes into competition for the same revenues. Old products will be not popular because which become harder to sell. Obsolescence, therefore depends not only on time, but also on competition, in the same time of business. It seems technological innovation can avoid obsolescence occurrence to old products to raise which competitive ability to the same markets. However, there was hardly an element in the competitive cost structures of conversion processes which was not disturbed in a way which differentiated country form country, industry from industry and firm from firm, such as technological innovation to any old products, which production of factor cost structures is the same basically.

● What is the benefit to process of technological innovation in the factor of production?

The term "innovation" is used to describe the deliberate process by which a new product or process comes to be sold in the market. Technology innovation can be applied to conversion processes, which requires the use of energy, or their products, which have an economic energy content. It is therefore a function of all the forces which shape markets: manufacturing, processing, technology, buying, selling, information, prices costs etc. So an innovating organization may be a whole company or it may be an individual. Other forms of innovation (production of factor) relate to the sale of services within what defines as the facilitiation system. That sort of exchange is not specifically considered to be one production of factor, because it involves different adoptation processes and response times, and doesn't of itself add to the quantity of products or utilities sold.

However, invention can not be defined to one production of factor and it is to be distinguished to innovation. We can describe invention is as the process of discovering something completely new, i.e. a new fact or relationship. It is an important scientific advance. Invention enlarges the scope of man's awareness, but it doesn't necessarily have direct economic value in itself. If it is sold, it is the sale of an idea, an exchange of a little creativity for an incentive within the facilities system. It isn't marketed as a new product of a conversion process. No energy of conversion is involved. The great majority of inventions do not enter into the economic process and which do not become innovations until that happens.

If the change of scope results in a new process for making a product or utility which is already being sold, this can't be differentiated from the existing product or utility in the market concerned. To be successful the new process must make it at lower unit cost than existing process. The result then is that either the price of the product fulls and processes to improve are imposed to competition or more net revenue is accumulated. So the aims of the factors of technological innovation production include: The introduction of a process for making at a lower unit cost a non-differentiated product which is sold into a commodity market, and the development and sale of a differentiated product which will draw buyers away from other markets, or draw money into the market which would not otherwise have been spent.

The nature of technological innovation how causes factor of production. The process of technological innovation is the arrangement of materials at the elementary, say atomic or molecular level, or of components or the design of new machines, or of the relative positions of components, for example, the location of nodes in networks. There are the three levels at which the scope of the economic process may be changed. However, technological innovation can't seem without some change in the way materials ae ordered. It follows that all technological innovation flows initially from some change in a conversion process. Thus technological in the result of investment in conversion processes, where investment is defined as laying down fixed assets and so it requires a change in the use of energy consumed during conversion to make useful products. The flexible manufacturing system themselves are examples of the third level of innovation, the spatial arrangement of components and hence the link between them. Patterns of communication have changed and are continue to change as a result of new technoloby in the use of energy and the convergence of computer, data maipulation and telecommunication. Flexible manfacturing systems manufacture components in rather than having them made by supplies industries and transported to an assembly plant in batches. The new arrangements reduce both the time of reponse to market changes and all the skills of components which are needed to give flexibility of response in conventional systems , i.e. they give economy of scope.

In the terminology which have developed above, the behavioral effects may be considered as adjustment of the scope of the sellers and buyers organizations as the process of acceptance of the innovation in the market proceed. Costs and risks in technological innovation, innovation requires the commitment of resources over a long period, and it is therefore subject to the same kind of risks as any investment in conversion processes. The most obvious risk is that the technological difficulties are in the initial concept, with the result that no returns will be earned and the resources sunk in the investment may have been wasted. There is a set of market-related reasons why technological success may not result in an innovation. By the time, the new process or product is ready for the market, the demand for it may have receded or may never have materialised. This may be the result of fulfiment of the potential users' needs by another technology, i.e. the innovation may be technologically obsolete before it may be because of a change of fashion or styles of living.

Two conclusions may be drawn, firstly, the product manufacturer has a good foresight and understanding is needed when undertaking projects which consume large amount of capital, or it may result in gross waste, because the future is always uncertain, however, the analysis, secondly, there is a limit to the rate of constructive innovation in an economic system, the ratio at which the system can accumulate. Hence, some product manufacturer will feel the technological innovation can be a good production of factor , such as a cost advantage is termed a competitive advantages. It is a broader term than the comparative advantages of traditional economy because of does not depend on a favorable climate or an abundance of natural resource. It is developed and maintained entirely by the skills of the people in the firms which are involved.

Technology is like on the economic process, because once knowledge about transforming inputs into outputs has been obtained, and especially after it has been implemented, it doesn't disappear. Technological innovation moves the whole process. Thus, economy of scope confer permanent advantages on those who have them. Economy of scope is to be obtained from all the elements of the economic process which change with time and these are suspectible to improvement, whether as separate elements. They involve people, and their capacity to learn and improve, and material in all their different forms.

Innovation is the process by which new products' processes methods or services are created. Innovation offers added value for and users by providing better and/or cheaper functionality than previous options. Innovation combines changes in technology, business models, organization etc. The basic idea may be a new technical solutions, a new business model or a change in organization. In a competitive economy, no business can survive long term without updating its products and services or the ways in which are produced or delivered. Innovation policy must promote renewal across all business sectors and not just focus on high technological industries.

Since most innovations are complex and each subsystem has its own limitation , an important part of the innovation process is finding the right balance between conflicting demands. In most cases, there are several possible ways of providing a new function to users, or possible applications of a new technology. Which combination of features the market will prefer can't be predicted with any certainty. Whether the origin was a market opportunity on a new technological capability to one part of the production of factor to the product.

Innovation integrates knowledge from a number of different fields: technology, marketing, design, economic etc. In the production of factor view, it is hard to collect all the necessary competences in a single organization. Because technological products need to be updatd to keep competition in market. Thus, innovation has become a process of constant with suppliers and competitors, with consultants and with academic researchers. In the production of factor view, the capacity to innovate depends on how well different parts of this system are adapted to each other and how well they work together.

Today, the relationship between science and innovation is more complex and interdependent. Science-based technologies, such as microelectronics or biotechnology could not have been developed without scientific understanding, but modern science is equally dependent on advanced technology. Economists tend to prefer technology performance standards, but these risk favouring marginal improvements to existing technologies when discouraging more radical, long term solution. Also, economists tend to think of innovation as a production processes. A more production describes innovations as an experimental learning proces in which organizations and individuals build new competence. This term "research-based competence" is rather than " science-based knowledge or "scientific information".

I shall argue that economists' active process is a better way of think about the relationship between industry and academic research. Whether can the production of factor of technological innovation make use of the tools and results of research in addressing real world problem to manufacture any technological products? This main concern at the time was whether research and innovation were essentially different activities which should be supported in different ways or whether it was important to deal with both aspects together since which were interdependent.

However, innovation is a process of searching, experimenting and learning. Consumers can learn about how new products, processes and services are created, how firms build competence for this and what information sources which use. So, I feel technological innovation ought be one part of production process or production of factor to some manufacturers. Such as, searching is needed for better ways of doing worth which things. Experimenting is needed because consumers can't seen in advance the best way of accomplishing a desired outcome or indeed what users really want or need. Learning is needed because actors involved in an innovation process will learn from it. The kind of learning which changes consumers' ability to solve future challenges and opportunities. However, economists often think of innovation is as a production prcocess, where knowledge transformed into a new product. We measure research and development investment, relating these to outcomes in the form of patents, new products and productivity or economic growth. Innovations are not just new technological products or processes, it also mentions organizational innovations, new distribution channels, new business models etc. In fact, it is often misleading to think about technical or organizational innovation as separate processes. Most innovations combine changes in technology, business models organization etc. in production process.

What kinds of product can belong to high technological manufacturing. For example, the world's most advanced steel plants and paper mills can never be classified as high technology because of their complementary need for high levels of investment in fixed capital, and aerospace manufacture is classified as medium technology. The standard definition of high technology measures research and development intensity not the generation or use of advanced technology as such. A far better measure is the proportion of scientists, engineers and highly qualified technicians in the labor force. For computer industry example, innovations in the field of rabotic manufacturing, nanotechnologies and human genetics research all have been enabled by low cost computational and control capabilities supplied by computers and software. Reducing the cost of software important objectives of the U.S. software industry. However, the complexity of the software industry to support the U.S. is computerized economy is increasing at an alarming rate. Software nonperformance and failure are expensive. In actuality many factors contribute to the quality issues facing the software industry. These include marketing strategies, limited liability by software vendors, and decreasing returns to testing.

At the core of these issues is the difficulty in defining and measuring software reliability, usability, efficiency, maintenability and portability. Information problems are further complicated by the fact that even with substantial testing, software developers don't truly know how their products with perform until who encounter real scenarios. The similiar industries with need have technological innovation in the productive process (production of factor), such as automotive and aerospace equipment manufacturers and related electronic communications equipment manufacturers. Quality is defined as attribute factor to different kinds of software product. Defining the attributes of software quality and determining the metrics to access the relative value of each attribute are not formalized processes. Because users place different values on each attribute depending on the product's use, it is important that quality attributes be observable to consumers. The technological innovation is one production of factor to software industry. Due to software attributes have those accurateness, interoperability, security, reliability (maturity, recoverability); usability (understandability, learnability, operability); efficiency (time behavior, resource behavior); maintainability (analyzability, changeability, stability, testability); portability (abaptability, installability, replaceability). It seems that due to software attribute have these characteristics, so it causes technological innovation is one production of factor to software industry.

Nowadays, human needs have been increasing, external factor can influence some industries cause technological innovation is one production of factor need. Together, these tends are going to reshape now human live and work, reorganize our social, economic and political institutions and redistribute power and reward in society. In the longer term, as machine learning and computer power intelligence technological innovation needs from consciousness, as machine learning and computer from consciousness, as improving health technologies allow for biological enhancements and species divergence, and as the final frontier is also needed by space travel, technological and social transformation will increasingly change what is means to be human. However, human have to better understand how our world is changing and by what forces those changes are driven . So, because human have high living quality needs, so it causes many new products have technological innovation to manufacture new product or to raise high quality need to satisfy our daily life. It will cause of factor to some products.

The technological innovation factor can influence the economic of the pork meat production in agricultural industry. For example, the economy of the pork meat production on a farm has been carried out with the help of the method of production functions (factor- product and factor-factor). The influence of the weight of an animal on the daily growth tells us that the growth is increased with the increse of the entry weight to 19kg and with the exit weight of the fattened animal of 100 kg. So, the relationship between the daily growth and the feed costs by a feeding day shows us the tendency of than increase of a daily growth with the increase of the feed costs, e.g. with the increase of labor inputs to 2.6 hours/100 kg of the live weight and the increased profit to 29 monetary units. Labor productivity grows with the increase of the capacity usage to 87% and then it decrease. The economy of agricultural production considerably depends on the development of cattle-breeding as a natural capacity of transforming plant products into high quality cattle products. Cattle-raising production influences the food quality, the development of food production industry, the output of high quality and healthy safe product and the development of agricultural economy. So, it seems technological innovation can be a production of factor to influence farm agricultural industry to assist farmers to apply high, e.g. agricultural technology (skills) produces high quality and tastic of farming met to satisfy consumers' diet needs.

Growth of total factor productivity (TFP) can provide society with an opportunity to increase the welfare of people. In particular, in the simplest framework, change in labor productivity factor depends on change (TFP) and capital deepening. How to change TFP? I shall suppose the technological innovation method is a factor to reduce labor cost, but it can raise labor productivity and products or goods of quality to satisfy consumers' needs in competitive market. Economists often define the knowledge economy as production and services based on knowledge-intensive activities tht contribute to an accelerated pace of technical and scientific technology, as well as rapid absolescence. Knowledge is now recognized as the driver of productivity and economic growth, leading to a new focus on the role of information, technology and learning in economic performance. In the knowledge-based economy, innovation is driven by the interaction of producers and users in the exchange of both codified and tacit knowledge: This interactive model has replaced the traditional linear model of innovation. The knowledge-intensive and high technology, economy tends to be the most dynamic in terms of output and employment growth. Changes in technology and particularly the advent of information technologies are making educated and skilled labor more valuable, and unskilled labor less. So, the technological innovation production of factor will bring skilled labor needs, more and unskilled labor needs less.

Although, it can maximize the benefits of technology for productivity, but it can raise unemployment number of non-skillful labor, because the high technological product firms will choose to dismiss the non-skillful labor and will employ skillful labor when innovation which decide to apply technological innovation method to produce whose products. For example, output and employment are expanding fastest in high technology industries, such as computers, electronic and aerospace. Also, knowledge-intensive service sectors, such as online education, communication and information(long distance call) are growing even faster, such as internet shopping technological business can be production of factor to let universities can teach students from internet, such as distance learning. Internet can be used to adventise and sell products from businessman individual website more easily. Also, mobile can use internet to do same benefits, such as laptop or desktop kinds of high technological computer products. It seems technological benefits can attract consumer individual consumption more easily. So, skillful biased technical change is a shift in the production technology that favors skilled over unskilled labor by increasing its relative productivity and therefore, its relative demand. In fact, skill-biased technical change is a shift in the production technology (factor of production that favors skilled, e.g. more relative productivity) and therefore, its relative demand.

In fact, the competition advantages of a company strongly depends on its possibility to benefit from innovational activities. Understanding the factors how which affect product and process innovation and their effort is necessary to be proved why innovational activities can be the one part production of factors to some new products. It has close relationship between product and business processes innovation and industry maturity and customer needs (demand) technological opportunities and investment attractiveness and company size and export orientation. These external and internal factors can influence innovational activities to some new products.

Nowadays, fast technology development, combined with the globalization and fast changes in with the globalization and fast changes in customer demand, implies that a competitive advantage of a company. So, companies will spans great effort in beating the competition innovations have a vital influence on economic development of a country. On the macro level, innovations have a vital influence on economic development that innovations are more and more present both a developed and developing countries that wish to grow developing countries that wish to grow fast and become developed. If we simply categorize companies all innovative or non-innovative. Among different innovation's categorizations is developed by researchers, the most important are: classification according to the type of innovation to degree of innovativity, innovations can be classified as incremental, semi-radical and radical innovations (Davila et al 2006), who indicates that radical innovations potentially offer huge profits and competitive advantage, but demand considerably high risk level, much company effort need and resource engagement. Otherwise, incremental innovations have more modest returns, but demand lower risk level, level of efforts and resources and are generally more successful. Finally, semi-radical innovations are somewhere between the two of them.

According to (Christensen 2003) explained to an innovations can be sustaining and disruptive. Sustaining innovations can be placed in the whole range from incremental to radical and discuptive are either semi-radical or radical. Sustaining innovations are those that improve existing products or process, disregarding the degree of improvement. Disruptive innovations create a huge growth offering a new of performances which has even it is inferior from the start comparing to existing technologies' performances a potential to become superior. Companies are advised to accept what is the best for their situation and design innovational processes, develop aptitudes, allocate resources and form partnerships in compliance to that decision.

In fact, many external and internal factors can affect companies chose product innovations, because process, innovations or their combination, e.g. factors include industry maturity, customer needs and expectations , technological opportunities, investment attractiveness, intensity of cmpetition, company size, origin of ownership and export orientation. In the industry maturity stage, as a market matures and customer needs become defined in a better way, companies transfer the focus of their competition to expenses and economy of range investing more in business processes in order to make them more effective and more efficient. Customer needs and expectations are essential for process innovations that improve process effectiveness. Orientation to customers and their satisfaction are well-known concept in the field of a total quality management.

The point of view that market demand presents the main determine the rate and activities of an invention because each rational company that tends to make profit is responsive to economic stimuli . According to Schmookler (1962) demand growth is prior to the growth in innovative activites, i.e. market requests guarantee stimuli for companies to innovate and take up new technologies. This concept is popularly called " market pull" in a sense that a market pulls innovations.

● How technological innovation excites knowledge consumers buying desire

I shall give evidences to explain why technological innovation can be one kind of production factor to some technological product manufacture industry as well as it can excite knowledge to raise consumers buying desire nowadays. Nowadays, we are entering the knowledge based economy stage.

Knowledge is now recognized as the driver of productivity and economic growth, leading to new focus or the role of information technology and learning in economic performance. The knowledge based economy and its relationship is as traditional economics, as reflected in " new growth theory". Because every technological product manufacturer needs workers to acquire a range of skills and to continuously adapt these skills underlines the " learning economy". The importance of knowledge and technology diffusion requires better understanding of knowledge networks and " national innovation systems".

Firstly, knowledge-based economies which are directly based on the production, distribution and use of knowledge and information. The is reflected in the trend in growth in high technology investment, high technological industries, move highly-skilled labor and associated productivity gains. Also required is tacit knowledge including the skills to use and adapt codified knowledge-based economy, innovation is driven by the interaction of producers and users in the exchange of both codified and tacit knowledge.

Employment in the knowledge-based economy is characterized by increasing demand for more highly skilled workers. The knowledge-intensive and high-technology tend to be the most dynamic in terms of output and employment growth. The science system, essentially public research laboratories and institutes of highest education, carries out key functions in the knowledge-based economy, including knowledge production, innovative technology. So, the traditional functions of producing new knowledge through basic research and educating new generations of scientists and engineers with its newer role of collaborating with industry in the transfer of knowledge and technology. For example, our societies tend to research institutes and academic increasingly have industrial partners for financial as well as innovative purposes, but most combines this with their essential role in more generic research and education.

In general, our understanding of what is happening in the knowledge-based economy is constrained by the extent and quality of the available knowledge-rated indicators. So, available knowledge-rated indicated. So, development of indicators of the knowledge-based economy must start with improvements to more traditional input indicators of research and development expenditures and research personal. Better in indicators are also needed of knowledge stocks and flows, particularly relating to the diffusion of information technologies, in both manufacturing and service sectors; social and privates rates of return to knowledge investments to the impact of innovation technology in productivity and growth.

However, knowledge is such as human being (human capital) and in innovative technology has always been central to economic development. When human is entering the 21 ST century, our output and employment are expanding tastes in high technology industries, such as computers, electronics and aerospace investment is thus being directed to high-technology products and services, particularly information and communicating technologies. Computers and related equipment are the fastest growing component of tangible investment. Equally important are more intangible investments in research and development, the training of the labor force, computer software and technical expertise. Hence, it causes employment is growing in high technology, science-based sectors ranging from computers to pharmaceuticals. Also, research and development causes manufacturing sector is losing jobs. Due to those jobs are more highly skilled and pay higher wages than those in lower technology sectors (e.g. textiles and food processing). Knowledge-based jobs in service sectors are also growing strongly. Indeed, non-production or knowledge workers those who don't engage in the output of physical products, are the employees in most demand in a wide range of activities from computer technicians, through physical therapists to marketing specialists.

Economists continue to search for the foundations of economic growth. Traditional, " production functions" focus on labor, capital , materials and energy, land; however, knowledge and technology are external influence on production. Analytical approaches are being developed. So, that knowledge can be included more directly in production functions. Investment in knowledge can raise productive capacity of the other factors of production as well as transform them into new products and processes from innovative technology.

According to the neo-classical production function, returns diminish is as more capital is added to the economy an effect which may be offset, however, by the flow of new technology. In new growth theory, knowledge can raise the returns on investment, which can contribution to the accumulation of knowledge. Technological change can also raise the relative marginal productivity of capital through education and training of the labor force, investment in research and development and the creation of new managerial structures and worth organization. In fact, incorporating knowledge into standard economic production functions is not easy task, as this factor defies some fundamental economic principles, such as that of scarcity, knowledge is intangible, but labor, capital, land, equipment etc. production of factors which can be tangible or measured. However, some kinds of knowledge can be easily reproduced and distributed at lower cost to abroad set of users, which tends to undermine private ownership. Knowledge is a much broader concept than information, which is generally the " know-what", and "know-why" components of knowledge. There are also the types of knowledge which come closet to being market commodities or economic resources to be fitted into economic production functions.

Knowledge can divide know-why and know-how both kinds of concept. Know-why means to scientific knowledge of the principles and laws of nature. This kind of knowledge underlines technological development and product and process advances in most industries. The production and reproduction of know-why is often organized in specialized organizations, such as research-laboratories and universities. Otherwise, know-how means to skills or the capability to do something. Business judging market prospects for a new product or a personnel manager selecting and training staff have to use their know-how. The same is true for the skilled worker operating complicated machine tools. Finally, knowledge-who becomes increasingly important. Know-who involves information about who knows what and who know how to do what. It involves the make if possible to get access to experts and use their knowledge efficiently. So, knowledge economy brings those conditions to our societies. One hypothesis is that globalization and international competition have led to decrease relative demand for less-skilled workers of the phenomenon; an alterative explanation is that innovative technology change has become more strongly biased in favor of skilled workers, changes in firm behavior is as the main reason for falling real wages for low-skilled workers. Thus, innovative technology and knowledge economy has close relationship to cause knowledge workers can bring high technological products of production of factor in technological product manufacture industry.

Secondly, it is the internal skill biased technical change influences. Skill-biased technical change is a shift in the production technology, that flavors skilled over unskilled labor by increasing its relative productivity and , therefore, its relative demand of innovative technology of production factor. The direction of technical changes i.e. whether new capital complements skilled or unskilled labor may be determined by innovators' economic incentives shaped by relative prices, the size of the market and institutions.

Economic theory views the production technology as a function describing that a collection of factor inputs can be transformed into output, and it defines technical change as a shift in the production of function. In fact, given who observed movements of the production function only concentrates on , such as land supply, labor numbers, equipment supply, capital demand factors. Therefore,To make sense of these recent developments, the concept of factor biased technical change can be another production of factor to influence the new technical products quantities change. For example, the timing of the rise in the skill premium has changed the rapid diffusion of information and communication technologies in the workplace environment in any high technological industry generally nowadays. For example, expenditures in information processing equipment and software, is as a share of U.S. private non-residential fixed investment, rose from 6% in 1960 year to 40% in 2000 year. At the heart of those dynamic change.

This is an improvement in the quality and productivity of all those equipment products, relying heavily on semiconductors like computers, software and switching equipment underlying much of communication technology. In the early adoption phase of a new technology, that those who adapt more quickly can reap some benefits. As time goes by, there will be enough makers learning how to work with the new technology to offset the wage differential. Note the difference with the hypothesis set, where the effect of capital deepening on the skill premium is permanent. Also, information technologies production of factor can reduce costs of data storage, communication, monitoring and supervision activities within the firm which causes a shift towards a new organizational design. In particular, the layers in the hierarchical structure can be reduced, so that the organization of the firm becomes "flatter". So, workers no longer perform routinized, responsible for a wide range of tasks within teams. Therefore, adaptable workers verses at multi-tasking activities benefits is a factor of production to reduce internal cost of any firms.

Due to technological innovation causes the layers in the hierarchical structure can be reduced, so that the organization of the firm becomes "flatter". How technological innovation can influence internal skill biased technical change to orgnizational structure. Development behavioral means it is through managment theory. So, high technological skillful organization will choose to apply theory x more than theory y because this technological innovation will reduce some unskillful staffs and give more effort and duties to those skillful staffs to use high technological skill to do whose jobs daily and who will feel lazy and unhappy to do extra more technological jobs. Theory x assumptions are the average human being dislike of work and work avoid if who can, most people must be controlled, directed or threatened with punishment to adequate effort to action organization objective; otherwise, theory y assumptions are people like to use physical and mental effort to work as natural as play and rest, human being dislike work, a source of satisfaction, threat of punishment are not being effort. Hence, technological innovation can cause organizations to change whose structure and skill staffs need to do more jobs. It causes employer need to give extristic and intrinsic motivations to satisfy whose skillful staffs needs to raise efficiency, e.g. giving more tangible reward, as salary, benefit, security, promotion, good contract of condition of work service, comfortable workplace environment as well as using one ability to achieve who feel apprecation, positive being treating of psychological satisfactory needs.

In technological innovation of organization structure, the management committee needs to concern whose skillful technological labor individual psychological needs. Because technological innovation is one important production of factor and it has close relationship between motivation and staff individual efficiency and productivity. As Maslow's hierarchy of needs indicates people (staffs) mean having satisfied to achieve motivation behavior, the lowest love is basic physiological, the need for food, as salary, safe working condition, then is job security, benefit. Next is friendship at work group, after is promotion, payment increasing, high status of job title. Finally is achievement in work advancement opportunitie creative task in related aspect at work motivation. Hence, after the traditional non-technological innoviation of organization changed the technological innovation of organizational structure, management needs to concern that motivation is needed to develop of behavioral through contributed to management theory. Every organiztion manageer needs to know what its team staffs whose indvidual needs, it includes extrinsic needs, e.g. salary, promotion, security as well as intrinsic needs, e.g. achievement, appreciaton. If the employees feel extrinsic needs are more than intrinsic needs, the managers can consider what extrinsic needs, the managers can consider what extrinsic needs of whose employee individual need. If the employee feels intrinsic needs are more than extrinsic needs, the manage can consider what intrinsic needs the employee individual actual need in order to motivate the skillful worker to work efficiently and raising productivity.

After changing the technological innovation of organizational structure, the management needs to concern how to plan to raise its productivity from its production of factor of technological innovation. Planning is looking ahead, control is looking back, every organization must need strategic plan, operative plan and tastic plan for every department to give aim for its mission objectives. Then it needs to achieve its any short term plans or long term plans efficiently, e.g. how to achieve to produce and to sell 5,000 computers sale objective or how to increase to achieve 20% profit or productivity objective from 10% within one year. So, after the technological innovation production of factor influences the organization needs to find reasons what how to influence it can not achieve these new objectives within one year. Then, it needs to find reasons and revises to solve challenges to control it can achieve it's planning objectives. For example, SWOT method indicates what its internal strengths and weaknesses, external threats and opportunities are. To aim achieve its planning strategic plan every year. Before the organization is not technological innovation, it can't have control is looking ahead, due to planning is looking back because organization can;t know what it's mission and objectives can't achieve to revise if it has no any strategic plan, operational plan and tactical plan for top, middle and low level to let different department managers to know what it's mission and objectives are planned to achieve before the organization has not changed the technological innovation of organizational structure in the year. Besides, after the technological innovation changed the organizational structure. The management needs to concern how to implement it's strategies effectively. The technological innovation of organization needs to change its old long term strategic plan to be new long term strategic plan in the top level, e.g. one year what is its new mission for its technologcial innovation, e.g. Apple brand of computer company needs to innovate its old style computer design to know how to adapt the young client group needs (demand) in this competitive computer technological product industry.

Finally, after innovative organizational structure, mangement needs to concern how to raise skillful labor individual productivity and efficiency, due to who need to increase more effort to do their jobs after technological innovation. I shall indicate on job training method. The advantages on limitations of different approaches to on the job training include the company needs to spend extra time and resources to train staffs or workers to work, when who are on the regular work time. Hence, it will lose staffs to do regular job duties, due who needs to learn how to do their job. So the employer needs to pay higher salary to every job trainer for long term if it needs to train many skillful labor after technological innovation. It can't ensure whether the training employees can work efficiently and know who are not the right staffs to get training. Hence, it will employ the staffs who are not right staffs to accept job training riskly if the mangement have not evaluate who have effort to be train to raise whose productivity and testing personal effort of evaluation is more important to the job trainers.

Finally, I shall indicate what the change is as exogenous or endogenous factor in the production function model to cause innovative technology to produce new technological product in manufacture industry. Although, economic theory firstly treated technology change is as a residual, the unexplained part remaining after the contribution of an increased quantity and quality of capital, labor and natural resources in output growth have been accounted for. However, the theory of economic growth reconsidered recently the nature of technological change and the concept of knowledge. Therefore, the new growth economic theory includes research and development is as a factor of influence in the macroeconomic models.

The endogenous or exogenous nature of technological change refers to its source: endogenous is internal to the national economy, being created by domestic private or public enterprise, when exogenous change is external originating from foreign sources. So, it seems research and development workforce is as new factor in the production function model. Although, technological progress, managerial improvements and innovation in general are nowadays largely regarded as key contributors to economic growth. Schumpeter (1939) defines technical progress in terms of production function, which describes the way the production output varies according to the quantity and quality of the input factors. So, the technological change represents the factor that shifts the production function.

From the theoretical viewpoint, it has difficult to separate knowledge from the other factors of the production function. The total labor factor productivity is usually estimated by output the capital and labor factors, weighted by their specific shares. Under perfect competition, the price of the production factors is equal to their marginal productivity, hence, their shares in outputs are equal to their exponents from the production function.

Otherwise, from the empirical point of view, there are difficulties of measurement, especially in the case of value added and research-development variables. So, from all available data on research and development input and outputs, research and development expenditures are most frequently used, along with the number of patents, the technological balance of payments, machinery and tools inputs etc. costs to measure of input in innovation.

Furthermore, the exponents of the new growth theory indicates modeled knowledge is as an output quality of the research and development sector and proved that contrary to the neoclassical conclusions of the diminishing-returns technology, the introduction of the human capital changes the production function into one with increasing returns. Thus, it seems total research and development expenditures are used in this model as a measure of total investments (material and intangible) in the research and development sector. However, in many studies, the research and development stock is calculated as the accumulated value of research and development expenditure after depreciation, a procedure which implies the assumption that all of the research and development expenditure certainly and that it's stock depreciates with a certain fixed rate. Since, long time-series data on R & D are rarely available, other studies assume that the growth rate of R & D expenditure to R & D stock is stable. Hence in innovation technological industry, the labor production factor can be divided into two components total employees population outside the research development sector and the number of employees in research and development. The same types of division was applied to the capital production factor.

Reference

Christensen, C.M. (2003) " the innovator's dilema", Harpercollins, New York.

Davila, T., Epstein, M. J., Shelton.R. (2006) " Making innovation work: How to manage it, measure it and profit from it". Warton school publishing,

New Jersey.

Schmookler, J., (1962) " Economic sources of incentive activity, " the journal of economic history. vol. 22
, no. 1 (Mar. 1962), 1-20.

Schumpeter, J., A. (1939), business cycles: A Theoretical Historical And Statistical Analysis Of Capitalist Processes, New York: Macmillan.

CHAPTER TWO

How applying economy theories learn technological consumer purchase behaviors

● Cultural factor raises Afican technological products demand

The technological product shortage economic problem – sometimes called the basic or central technological product purchase problem – asserts that a conuntry has many students or working people need to buy any technologial products to use in society, but the technological product resources are insufficient to satisfy all technological product consumers' wants and needs in short time, e.g. different kinds of laptops, desktop, software, television, radio, waching machine. Economics involves the study of how to allocate resources in conditions of scarcity However, viewing economics as the study of how society allocates resources can lead to conflation of normative economic planning and empirical study of how economic agents operate in these conditions. This technological products shortage challenge will cause in the developing countries, e.g. Africa. Because African can not manufacture any high technologica products, it needs to import any technological products from other technological products countries, e.g. US, UK. If Afica had many students or working people whose need to buy computers for working aspect or learning aspect, or buying washing machines to wash clothers to replace hand, due to their cultural improvement, then it will cause African feel to buy any kinds of high technological products needs or demand , then technological products supply number will increase to Africa market in possible. Then, cultural improvement will be one factor to cause one poor or developing countries people feel to need to use many high technological products in their daily lives.

In mainstream neoclassical economics, it is assumed that humans pursue their self-interest, and that the market mechanism best satisfies the various wants different individuals might have. These wants are often divided into individual wants (which depend on the individual's preferences and purchasing power parity) and collective wants (which are the wants of entire groups of people). Things such as food and clothing can be classified as either wants or needs, depending on what type and how often a good is requested. So, such as African technological product market. When African feel their basic eating need and living need can satisfy, they have enough houses to live and enough food to buy to eat. Due to they had been improved their culture level by high education learning channel. Then, they need learn the developed countries people's daily living habits, e.g. learning to use washing machines to replaces hands to wach cloths, learn to use computer to read e-books, or distance learning learning method, or purchase high quality televisions to watch at home ,or purchase smart phones to replace moiles. So, African 's living habits change is due to their cultures are improved from education.

However, economists have sometimes characterized "how" to produce as a "technological problem" of efficiency whereas the allocation of what is produced is an "economic problem". In a free market, the "how" of production and allocation of resources is distributed among economic agents. In a centrally planned economy, a principal decides how and what to produce on behalf of agents. Modern economies are often welfare capitalist with various regulations, which makes the economic system more equitable while retaining the distributed free market system. Due to human wants are unlimited, an infinite series of human wants remains continue with human life. Nobody can claim that all of his wants have been satisfied and he has no need to satisfy any further want. Everybody feels hunger at a time then other he needs water. Sometime one feels the desire of clothing then starts to feel the desire of having good conveyance. When all existing wants are satisfied then new wants starts to create in mind, so the series of wants remains continue till the last moment of life. So an economic problem arises because of existence of unlimited human wants. So, African will encounter technological products supply challenge if African's cultures are improved to influence they feel high technological products needs raise, because our global different countries high technological products purchasers are also changing their high technological products needed to be improved. So, when high technological products manufactuers concentrate on researching how to improve their any kinds of high technological products to satisfy gloabal different developed countries consumers needs. Then, they will reduce time and manufacuring number to the traditional past time high technological products. Consequently, the number of traditional past time invention of high technological products supply number will also decrease. Then, it will case the traditional past time high technological products can not supply enough number to satisfy African 's high technological products purchase needs, due to they concentrate their time and resource to invent or improve the other new kind and high technological products to satisfy global high technological products consumers more than African high technological products consumers' needs. Because resource and time is not enough, so high technological products manufacturers only can research more resource to invent or improve the traditional high technological products to satisfy the other countries' high technological products buyers needs more than Africa people needs.

● Problem of allocation of resources to bring African high technological products shortage challange

The problem of allocation of resources arises due to the scarcity of resources, and refers to the question of which wants should be satisfied and which should be left unsatisfied. In other words, what to produce and how much to produce. More production of a good implies more resources required for the production of that good, and resources are scarce. These two facts together mean that, if a society decides to increase production of some good, it has to withdraw some resources from the production of other goods. In other words, more production of a desired commodity can be made possible only by reducing the quantity of resources used in the production of other goods. So, when the high technological products manufacturers need to spend time and resource to decide either to manufacture the improved high technological products to satisfy other countries people needs or still manufacture the low quality high technological products to satisfy African needs more. Then, it will bring the low quality of high technological products shortage to Africa because when they decide to spend time and nervous and resource to improve their low quality high technologial products to satisfy other countries people need.

The problem of allocation deals with the question of whether to produce capital goods or consumer goods. If the community decides to produce capital goods, resources must be withdrawn from the production of consumer goods. In the long run, however, [investment] in capital goods augments the production of consumer goods. Thus, both capital and consumer goods are important. The problem is determining the optimal production ratio between the two. Such as this African high technological products needs case , although their cultures are improved to influence they feel more need to use high technological products, but when the high technological product manufactuers feel resource is shortage to produce capital goods, e.g. machines, ships, cars. etc. Then , they will reduce to use more resources to manufacture the high techological consumer goods, e.g. computer, smart phone. So, it will influence African feel high technological products supply challenge when high technological manufactuers use more resource to produce technological capital goods more then technological consumer goods if they feel technological captial goods, e.g. machines are needed more in societies.

In fact, in our societies, resources are scarce and it is important to use them as efficiently as possible. Thus, it is essential to know if the production and distribution of national product made by an economy is maximally efficient. The production becomes efficient only if the productive resources are utilized in such a way that any reallocation does not produce more of one good without reducing the output of any other good. In other words, efficient distribution means that redistributing goods cannot make anyone better off without making someone else worse off. (See Pareto efficiency.) So, scientists will apply efficient distribution methods to help any countries to earn the absolute advantages when we buy and sell any kinds of products or food between ourselves countries, e.g. when US has good natural resource to grow any food, e.g. potato, wheat , vegetable, cotton , then US can export to sell to China, because China has no any farms to grow agriculture food to supply itself Chinese to eat. So, China must need to buy any agriculture food from US. Otherwise, China has cheap labor to supply to US any manufacturers to help them to manufacture their electronic products. SO, it has many US high technological product factories are built in China to let Chinese workers help them to produce their products because their wages are cheaper to compare US high technological products workers. So, comparative economic advantage will be choice to apply between US and China both countries in high technological product market. (Absolute advantage trade theory)

The inefficiencies of production and distribution exist in all types of economies. The welfare of the people can be increased if these inefficiencies are ruled out. Some cost must be incurred to remove these inefficiencies. If the cost of removing these inefficiencies of production and distribution is more than the gain, then it is not worthwhile to remove them.

● The problem of full employment of resources

In view of how to use available resources are fully utilized is an important one. A community should achieve maximum satisfaction by using the scarce resources in the best possible manner—not wasting resources or using them inefficiently. There are two types of employment of resources:

(1) Labour-intensive for high technological consumer product, e.g. smart phone, computer

(2) Capital-intensive for high technological capital product , e.g. machine

In capitalist economies, however, available resources are not fully used. In times of depression, many people want to work but can't find employment. It supposes that the scarce resources are not fully utilized in a capitalistic economy.

● The problem of economic growth

If productive capacity grows, an economy can produce progressively more goods, which raises the standard of living. The increase in productive capacity of an economy is called economic growth. There are various factors affecting economic growth. The problems of economic growth have been discussed by numerous growth models, including the Harrod-Domar model, the neoclassical growth models of Solow and Swan, and the Cambridge growth models of Kaldor and Joan Robinson. This part of the economic problem is studied in the economies of development.

● Needs and wants problems

Needs are things or material items of peoples need for survival, such as food, clothing, housing, and water. Everyone has a different needs and wants. Until the Industrial Revolution, the vast majority of the world's population struggled for access to basic human needs.

Wants are effective desires for a particular product, or for something that can only be obtained by working for it. While the fundamental needs of survival are key in the function of the economy, wants are the driving force that stimulates demand for goods and services. To curb the economic problem, economists must classify the nature and different wants of consumers, as well as prioritize wants and organize production to satisfy as many wants as possible.

However, high technological products are not essential needs to anyone, so wants are effective desires for a particular product,, e.g. laptop. The student can not must need to buy if he feels the laptop price is expensive, he can wait the laptop price goes down, then he can decide to buy later. So, the technological consumer product, e.g. laptop. The last month to the kind of laptop sale number is less, it can not represent the kind of lapop sale number is less. If its price can reduce little. Then it may increase the kind of laptop sale number in possible. Otherwise, needs are things or material items of peoples need for survival, such as food, clothing, housing, and water. So, people must need to buy food to eat , even they feel the kind of food price is increased because they will feel hunger. It is difficult to increase high technological product reason.

● Five bases problems of economy

In our societies , in general, our societies will have these similar problems The following points highlight the five basic problems of an economy. The problems are: 1. What to Produce and in What Quantities? 2. How to Produce these Goods? 3. For whom is the Goods Produced? 4. How Efficiently are the Resources being utilized? 5. Is the Economy Growing?.

Problem 1: What to Produce and in What Quantities?

The first central problem of an economy is to decide what goods and services are to be produced and in what quantities. This involves allocation of scarce resources in relation to the composition of total output in the economy. Since resources are scarce, the society has to decide about the goods to be produced: wheat, cloth, roads, television, power, buildings, and so on. Once the nature of goods to be produced is decided, then their quantities are to be decided. How many tones of wheat, how many televisions, how many million of power, how many buildings, etc. Since the resources of the economy are scarce, the problem of the nature of goods and their quantities has to be decided on the basis of priorities or preferences of the society.

If the society gives priority to the production of more consumer goods now, it will have less in the future. A higher priority on capital goods implies less consumer goods now and more in the future. But since resources are scarce, if some goods are produced in larger quantities, some other goods will have to be produced in smaller quantities. Suppose the economy produces capital goods and consumer goods. In deciding the total output of the economy, the society has to choose that combination of capital goods and consumer goods which is in keeping with its resources.

Problem 2: How to Produce these Goods?

The next basic problem of an economy is to decide about the techniques or methods to be used in order to produce the required goods. This problem is primarily dependent upon the availability of resources within the economy. If land is available in abundance, it may have extensive cultivation. If land is scarce, intensive methods of cultivation may be used. If labour is in abundance, it may use labour- intensive techniques; while in the case of labour shortage, capital-intensive techniques may be used.

The technique to be used also depends upon the type and quantity of goods to be produced. For producing capital goods and large outputs, complicated and expensive machines and techniques are required. On the other hand, simple consumer goods and small outputs require small and less expensive machines and comparatively simple techniques.

Further, it has to be decided what goods and services are to be produced in the public sector and what goods and services in the private sector. But in choosing between different methods of production, those methods should be adopted which bring about an efficient allocation of resources and increase the overall productivity in the economy.

Problem 3. For whom is the Goods Produced?

The third basic problem to be decided is the allocation of goods among the members of the society. The allocation of basic consumer goods or necessities and luxuries comforts and among the household takes place on the basis of among the distribution of national income. Whosoever possesses the means to buy the goods may have then. A rich person may have a large share of the luxuries goods, and a poor person may have more quantities of the basic consumer goods he needs.

Problem 4: How Efficiently are the Resources being Utilised?

This is one of the important basic problems of an economy because having made the three earlier decisions, the society has to see whether the resources it owns are being utilized fully or not. In case the resources of the economy are lying idle, it has to find out ways and means to utilize them fully.

Problem 5: Is the Economy Growing?

The last and the most important problem is to find out whether the economy is growing through time or is it stagnant. If the economy is stagnant at any point inside the production possibility curve, it has to be moved on to the production possibility curve PP whereby the economy now produces larger quantities of consumer goods and capital goods. Economic growth takes place through a higher rate of capital formation which consists of replacing existing capital goods with new and more productive ones by adopting more efficient production techniques or through innovations.

All of these economy problems will be our societies often causes to anyone feels need to solve problems in order to achieve our societies can have enough resources to satisfy our every day living.

● The Consumer Problem

Consumer theory is concerned with how a rational consumer would make consumption decisions. What makes this problem worthy of separate study, apart from the general problem of choice theory, is its particular structure that allows us to derive economically meaningful results. The structure arises because the consumer's choice sets are assumed to be defined by certain prices and the consumer's income or wealth. The consumer's problem is to choose that is most preferred or, equivalently, that has the greatest utility.

The assumption of perfect information is built deeply into the formulation of this choice problem, just as it is in the underlying choice theory. Some alternative models treat the consumer as rational but uncertain about the products, for example how a particular food will taste or a how well a cleaning product will perform. Some goods may be experience goods which the consumer can best learn about by trying ("experiencing") the good. In that case, the consumer might want to buy some now and decide later whether to buy more. That situation would need a different formulation. Similarly, if the agent thinks that high price goods are more likely to perform in a satisfactory way, that, too, would suggest quite a different formulation. Agents are price-takers. The agent takes prices p as known, fixed and exogenous. This assumption excludes things like searching for better prices or bargaining for a discount.

Hence , it seems that economic problems and consumer problems are similar, I feel that it is possible , economists can attempt to apply any economic theories to solve some consumer problems in some situations. They can find the accurate solutions when they can apply the suitable economic theories to solve the suitable consumer or economic problems in our societies. I shall indicate that how economists can apply the suitable economic theories to attempt to solve some consumer problems in our societies as below:

Demand And Supply Theory Solves Consumer Problems

What is economy rule predict consumer behaviour? Why and How does economist can apply economy rule to predict consumer behaviours? I shall explain the reasons as below:

Why does economic principle be the best to predict consumer behaviour. It may include these two reasons: The first focuses on the substantive domain of study, in this interpretation , economics is a social science devoted to understanding how the economy works. The second definition focuses on methods: economics is a way of doing social science, using particular tools. In this interpretation the discipline is associated with formal modelling and statistical analysis rather than particular hypotheses or theories about the economy. Therefore, economic methods can be applied to many other areas besides the economy, everything from decisions within the family to questions about political institutions.

High technolgical product increasing demand factor is similar to below public service or product increasing factor

● Demand and supply principle predict public transport tool passenger behaviour

Economists need to use the right economic ideas to predict consumer behaviour. So, Misuse the wrong economy ideas to predict consumer behaviours. It will do more wrong judgement to evaluate or predict why and how and when the country's consumer behaviours will change. It is every economist needs to consider issue. For example, the economy idea application of economic supply-demand principles to public transport. Different fares would give commuters with more-flexible hours the incentive to avoid peak travel times. They would allow passenger traffic to spread out over time, reducing the pressure on the public transport system when enabling even larger total passenger flow. IT aims to reduce traffic congestion, increased public-transport use, reduced car-bon emissions and cause air pollution and generated considerable revenue for the country's transport system. So, if the country can apply supply and demand economic principle to attempt to predict how many passengers number needs to catch transport tools to go to work or go to school or other activities. Then, it can predict how many bus, ferry, taxi, train, underground train, tram etc. different public transport tools to satisfy future public transport passengers' needs in society. So, this demand and supply principle is the comparative best rule to predict any kinds of public transport passengers' road needs, when they need to either go to school, go to office, go to leisure or shopping etc. different kinds of activities. So, applying the demand and supply principle to predict road and sea public transport passengers can help the country to reduce air pollution when they feel that they can find any public transport tools to catch any time conveniently , then it can encourage them to reduce car purchase desire. When many people choose to catch public transport tools, then it will reduce many cars number on the road. Then, air pollution will reduce as well as any public transport tools' income will also increase as well as traffic jam will also reduce. When the country can evaluate how many people choose to catch bus or taxi or ferry or train or underground train, or tram or train etc. different kinds of public transport tools, then the country can predict the more accurate public transport tools number to every kind of public transport tool to satisfy their journey needs. e.g. whether underground train or train or tram need to decrease or increase the frequent times or number to catch the volume of passenger in busy or non-busy time; or whether bus company has need to increase how much buses to catch the city location passengers when they are living in the city. Moreover, supply and demand principle can help any public transport tools to explain why their passengers number reduces in the year, it may due to fare charge is unreasonable, feeling uncomfortable to sit on the seat or air condition is poor in the transport tool environment, or there are no more seats because many there are much time is full passenger and no seat vacancy to provide to them to sit . So, supply and demand principle can help any kinds of public transport tools to find whether which is (are) the factor(S) can influence the current or last year passengers number reduce. Then, they can concentrate on improving their weaknesses to raise their service quality .

So, supply and demand principle can also help they to evaluate whether what their weakness are in order to improve to increase passengers number. They can do questionnaires to enquiry their passengers' response to evaluate whether which areas of services that they feel unsatisfactory. So, the different kinds of service satisfactory feeling to the passengers number data will be the main source to help the kind of public transport tool to analyse and conclude the results more accurate, then they can make the more accurate judgement to improve the of service. For example, the questionnaires indicate that the many passengers feel the bus fare is reasonable, but many passengers feel they can not find any seats to sit easily. So, it implies that the bus firm ought buy more buses or enlarges bus size and increases more seats in the enlarged buses. Then, it does not reduce its fare but it needs to find solutions to let passengers can find seats to sit in every bus more easily. But, if the questionnaires indicate that there are many passengers feel its fare is higher or unreasonable to compare other kinds of public transportation tools. Hence, it can avoid to spend more expenditure to increase bus number to the city, if the city has many passengers , they still choose bus to catch, but they feel its fare is too higher to compare other kinds of public transport tool. Then, it only needs to reduce its fare , it ought help it to increase passengers number. Hence, demand and supply principle is the most suitable economic method to evaluate any kinds of public transport system passenger needs in any country nowadays.

● Supply and demand and price elasticities principle predict oil energy user behaviour

The another case is that demand and supply principle can predict oil buyer behaviour to find whether what factors can cause the oil buyer individual need reduces. For example , a rise in production costs increases market prices and reduces quantities demanded and supplied. Or when, energy cost rise, utility bills increases and households fid extra ways of saving heating and electricity. But, others are nor. For example, whether a tax is imposed on the producers or consumer of a commodity, say oil has nothing to do with who ends up paying for it. The tax might be administered on oil companies, but it might be consumers who really pay for it through higher prices at the pump. Or the extra cost might be imposed on consumers in the form of a sale tax, but the oil companies might be forces to absorb it through lower prices. It all depends on the " price elasticities" of demand and supply. With the addition of extra assumption, this model also generates rather strong implications about how well markets work. In particular, a competitive market economy is efficient in the sense that it is impossible to improve one person's well-being without reducing somebody.

● Demand and supply principle can misuse to predict consumer behaviour when the two firms participate advertisement to promote their products in the same time

Why can demand and supply principle misuse to predict consumer behaviour when the two firms participate advertisement to promote their products in the same time ? I shall explain as below: Assume that two competing firms must decide whether to have a big advertising budget. Advertising would allow one firm to steal some of the other's customers. But when they both advertise, the effects on customer demand cancel out. The firms end up having spent money needlessly.

We might expect that neither firm would choose to spend much on advertising, but the model shows that this logic is off base. When the firms make their choices independently and they care only about their own profits, each one has an incentive to advertise, regardless of what the other firm does. When the other firm does not advertise, you can steal customers from it if you do advertise, when the other firm does advertise, you have to advertise to prevent loss of customers. So, these two firms end up in a bad equilibrium in which both have to waste resources. This market can not apply demand and supply principle to predict consumer behaviours because they depends advertisement to promote their products. If these two firms advertise their products in the same time. Then , it is not possible that if one firm increases it price and it will cause its customer number loss, due to its advertise can help it to attract customers to consider its product from television or radio or newspapers or magazine promotion channels. So, I suppose that these two firms decide to increase their price, when they advertise their products to let customers to know in the same time. They will not lose their customers or reduce their customers easily. Because their customers can be persuaded to choose to buy their products to compare other similar products in preference. So, their increasing price will not influence their customers number lose easily. It explains that demand and supply principle is not right to this case, so demand and supply principle can misuse to help them to predict consumer behaviours when they advertise their products in the same time. Also, demand and supply principle is not suitable to them to predict consumer behaviours when they advertise their products in the same time. They will do wrong prediction to their consumers purchase desire when they advertise their products in the same time.

ON conclusion, using these demand and supply and price elasticity techniques, economists derive specific prediction for how consumers choose which products to buy, how households save, how firms invest, how workers search for jobs, as well as for how these actions depend on the particulars. They can help them to predict job and consumption behaviours more accurate, it depends on whether the situation is right, such as both competition firms participate to advertise their products in the same time case, it is not right to apply above economic principle to predict consumer behaviours. They will get wrong prediction when they apply this principle to predict consumer behaviours.

However, demand and supply principle can predict below any one of these cases. I shall indicate as below:

The problem of need-based scholarships: Most systems for providing college scholarships are based on some definition of financial needs, with scholarships generally being given only to those students who must need financial help in order to attend school.

Is need, rather than academic ability, the best basic on which to choose those students who are to be encouraged to attend college? Which way of choosing who gets aids is the more just? Which is the more efficient ? Is the overall educational level of society increased more by giving financial aid to bright students or to needy students? Presumably the aid offers more leverage to needy students, since they all need the money in order to attend college, whereas, many of the bright students would attend college in any case. But is a smaller number of bright students the more important addition?

So, the school can apply demand and supply principle to predict whether how many parents feel need financial assistance and evaluate how much financial amount is the right to borrow. It aims to calculate how many parents feel real financial need and how much to lend to them in order to let these students to get the most fair financial assistance.

Assuming the school wish to use need as a basis, how does the school determines " financial need"?

Is need a function or parents' income? What, then , does the school about children of wealthy parents who are living independently of them and get no aid from parents? Should they be punished for their parents' wealth? But if they are given aid, won't all students, in order to get aid, claim to be independent of their parents?

Is need solely a matter of family income, or should not the school takes a family's financial obligations into account? Does not it make more sense to give aid to someone whose parents must put night more children through school than to someone from a family of five or one only with the same income? But in a possible parallel situations, should a family that carries mortgages on one or two large homes get preference simply because they do not have much money left to spend on college? Does doing this reward ?

Is there a difference between the case of night children and the case of the large mortgage? How should parents who are not married , but are living together and supporting their children jointly be counted? Most parents are supporter to their children , although they are married in possible.

So, the school needs to gather all these data to evaluate how many parents are not married or married or living with their children together, how much salary they earn as well as every family has how much children as well as whether they have mortgage for their houses. So, these number will be the financial education assistance demanders, but it does not represent their real financial needs. It is possible that someone does not feel any financial need, although their children apply financial assistance to your school. Then , your school needs to evaluate whether how much financial assistance can lend to every real financial need student family. It can not exceed your final financial expenditure budget (supply) , when your financial expenditure is not enough. SO, demand and supply principle can be applied to research this school real family financial demand to lend to the real financial need families and evaluate whether the reasonable financial amount to lend to every child family to study in your school.

● Supply and demand principle applies to immigration to decide wage case

A fascinating and important example of supply and demand, full of complexities, is the role of immigration in determining wages. If you ask people , they are likely to tell you that immigration into California or Florida US, surely lowers the wages of people in those regions. It is just supply and demand analysis of immigration. According to this analysis, of these to these two regions in US. Immigration in to a region shifts the supply curve for labor to the right and pushes down wages. Why has it relationship between immigration to US these two regions immigrant number and wage?

Careful economic studies cast doubt on this simple proposition, however, a recent survey of the evidence concludes:

The effect of immigration on the labor market outcomes of natives is small in US. There is no evidence of economically significant reductions in native employment. Most analysis, finds that a 10 percent increase in the fraction of immigrants in the population reduced native wages by a most 1%.

How can we explain the small impact of immigration on wages? The main mistake is to forget how mobile the American population is and that the impact of immigration on wages, we must examine the effect of new immigrants when the strength of the local economy and the number of native-born residents in a city are unchanged, that is , when these other things are held constant. Unless you exclude the effects other changing variables, you can not accurately predict the impact of immigration. The same principle holds in doing a supply0and demand analysis of any market. As much as possible, when you are examining the impact of a supply or demand shift, you must try to keep all other things constant.

● Rationing by prices

By determining the equilibrium prices and quantities of all inputs and outputs, the market allocated or rations out the scare goods of the society among the possible uses. Who does the rationing? A planning board? Congress or the president? BO, the marketplace, through the interaction of supply and demand, doe the rationing. This is rationing by the purse.

What foods are produces? This is answered by the signals of the market price. High oil prices stimulates oil production, whereas low food prices drive resources out of agriculture. Those who have the most dollars votes have the greatest influences on what goods are produced. All of these considers how demand and supply to the market.

For whom are goods produces? The power of the pursue indicates the distribution of income and consumption. Those with higher incomes end up with larger houses, more clothing, and linger vacations. When the most urgently felt needs get fulfilled through the demand curve.

Even, the how question is decided by supply and demand. When corn prices are low, it is not profitable for farmers to use expensive tractors and irrigation systems, and only the best land is cultivated. When oil prices are high, oil companies drill in deep offshore waters and employ novel seismic techniques to find oil.

IN sum , any thing needs through demands, interact with costs of goods, as reflected in supplies in our economic world. Hence, demand and supply theory ought be the most accurate method to help any businesses or governments to predict their shareholders behaviours when they will change as well as how and how their behaviours change.

Consumer choice theory solves consumer problems

What is 'consumer choice theory'?

'Consumer choice theory' is a hypothesis about why people buy things. Put simply, it says that you choose to buy the things that give you the greatest satisfaction, while keeping within your budget. At the heart of this theory are three assumptions about human nature.[1]

The first assumption is that when you shop, you choose to buy things based on calculated decisions about what will make you happiest. In economics language, this is known as utility maximisation (Economists really like to put quite simple concepts into long complicated terms.)

Secondly, the theory assumes that no matter how much you shop, you will never be completely satisfied. In other words, you will always be happier consuming a little bit more. This is known as the principle of non-satiation. Thirdly, even though you always get more happiness from more consumption, the amount of pleasure you get from each good decreases with the more you consume. So if you eat two ice creams rather than one, you get more overall pleasure, but the second ice-cream won't be as satisfying as the first. This is known as decreasing marginal utility.

Consumer choice theory has influenced everything from government policy to corporate advertising to academia. But the theory has been criticized for not being the most accurate description of how people actually make choices. A whole new branch of economics, called 'behavioral economics', has emerged essentially to use findings from psychology to disprove the assumptions behind consumer choice theory. This has also led others to argue that consumer choice theory is less about describing how we do actually behave, and is more about describing how people should behave.[3] In other words, by portraying people as self-interested shopaholics, economists are saying that is it okay and natural for us to be avid consumers.

● How to supply consumer choice theory to raise Consumer demand Marketing at Apple computer high technological producs

During US economy growth, Apply computer applies consumer choice theory to solve its computer buyers' choice problems among different kinds of brand computer competitors. Have you ever wondered why Apple is so successful? They were not the first company to invent the personal computer, portable music device, the tablet, the smartphone, software to download music, or the set-top box to name a few. Apple has amassed a brand loyal following like no other brand backed by significant sales, market share, and profitability. So, how does Apple do it? What's the secret behind their success?

Marketing using consumer behavior insight is how Apple succeeds. Even though Steve Jobs and Apple, did not use consumer research in the initial development of most products, consumer behavior plays a huge role in their marketing and ultimately the success of the company. Once a consumer purchases a product or downloads iTunes Apple has access to data the company leverages. Apple uses this information to gain significant insight into the consumer and what drives purchase behavior.

Consumer behavior marketing is an essential ingredient in the current business climate. The companies that apply this type of marketing well have a distinct competitive advantage that distances them from their rivals. Consumer behavior research is the primary driver at the core of any good strategy. Research provides actionable insight and ensures business success.

If you answer no to the following questions, this post is for you?

•Are you applying consumer behavior marketing currently?

•Have you conducted consumer behavior research within the last two years?

•Do you have consumer behavior marketing in your marketing plan with well-defined marketing strategies and tactics?

•Are you achieving the maximum results for your organization?

Every business has a target audience and consumer behavior marketing provides the fundamental methods for understanding your target. Consumer behavior research provides the underlying element that drives quality strategies and ensures business results.

"Marketing is understanding your buyers really, really well. Then creating valuable products, services, and information especially for them to help solve their problems."

The organizations that have an intimate understanding of their target audience possess a competitive advantage over those that do not. Establishing a one-to-one relationship and thorough knowledge of your target audience is a core responsibility for business in the 21st century and beyond. Regardless if you are B2B, B2C, B2G or a hybrid organization you have a target audience. The information in this post can be applied to any business type. This post focuses on Apple (B2C) employing consumer behavior marketing as a critical ingredient for their success.

Hence, Apply computer shops have several computer teachers to teach any visitors how to use its laptops, hen they enquire its any computer salespeople. Due to its salespeople had been trained to learn how to use the different kinds of laptops. So, anyone enquires them, they can answer their enquires concern any computer questions immediately. Then, they will feel Apple laptops are the first choice to compare other kinds of laptops brands. It is one salespeople answering strategies to persuade any Apple computer visitors to feel its any laptops are the first or preference choice to compare its competitors in this computer market, so customer choice economic theory is the most suitable strategy to solve Apple computer's customer individual purchase decision problem.

Microeconomics Models and Theories solve customer problems

Microeconomics is concerned with the economic decisions and actions of individuals and firms. Within the broad church of microeconomics, there are different theories that certain assumptions and expectations of economic behaviour. The most important theory is neo-classical theory, which places emphasis on free-markets and the assumption individuals are rational and seek to maximise utility. However, there are many critiques of the neo-classical model, arguing economics is more complex with issues of market failure and irrational behaviour.

Pre-classical microeconomic theory

Before, Adam Smith, economics was more disparate with no commanding overall theory. Philosophers like Aristotle and Plato made references to issues in economics such as division of labour. The dominant ideas, pre-classical economics, were based on theories of mercantilism – the idea a nation should try to accumulate gold.

Classical microeconomic theory

Classical microeconomic theory was developed by Adam Smith (Wealth of Nations, 1776) and later economists, such as David Ricardo The essential aspect of classical microeconomic theory include:

Adam Smith mentioned the 'invisible hand of the market.' He noted how when people act out of self-interest, markets tend to provide goods and services which are demanded by the population. It needed no central price setting, but market forces responded to changes in demand and supply, e.g. a shortage pushes up the price and causes demand to fall.

Smith also investigated topics such as the division of labour, specialisation and economies of scale. The early classical economists emphasised the importance of costs to firms and consumers.

Utility maximisation

An important development of classical economics towards the end of the nineteenth century is the concept of utility maximisation. The concept of utility was developed by philosophers/economists – Jeremy Bentham and John Stuart Mill. In microeconomic theory, it was believed a consumer will buy goods depending on the marginal utility (satisfaction) they get from the good. This theory assumes consumers are rational and seeking to maximise the satisfaction they get.

Neo-classical theory

Neo-classical theory is a modern re-interpretation of classical economics of the nineteenth century. Neo-classical theory places importance on markets, but developed new ideas, especially regarding utility and rational choice theory. Elements of neo-classical theory.

1. Market distribution of goods and services.

2.R ational choice theory. This is the idea individuals hold rational preferences and make rational choices; seeking to maximise their outcomes – be it profit, wages, consumption or investment.

3. People act independently and make use of available information.

4. Marginalism. In neo-classical economics, more emphasis was placed on concepts of marginal utility and marginal cost. We make choices depending on satisfaction we get from one extra unit of a good.

Economists such as Carl Menger, William Stanley Jevons and Marie-Esprit-Léon Walras. and Alfred Marshall developed ideas such as diminishing marginal utility. Many of these neo-classical economic theories were brought together in Alfred Marshall's very influential textbook, Principles of Economics. (1890)

•Note there is some blurring between classical economics and neo-classical economics.

•Neo-classical economics has also come to mean 'orthodox economic theory. To a large extent, it has incorporated new developments in microeconomics, such as theories of market failure, market structure and econometrics.

Theories of Market failure

Neo-classical economics has become associated with a belief in the efficiency of markets. However, microeconomic theory has also incorporated the criticisms and limitations of free-markets.

•Monopoly. Adam Smith was well aware of the problem of monopolies and how firms could use their market power to set excessive prices.

•Imperfect competition. In the 1930s, Joan Robinson developed a model of imperfect competition, an awareness many markets were somewhere between monopoly and perfect competition often assumed in neo-classical economics.

•Externalities. Developed by Arthur C.Pigou in The Economics of Welfare (1920) this is the awareness production and consumption decisions can have harmful (or positive) effects on third parties. Therefore, a free market can lead to overconsumption of demerit goods and negative externalities.

•Game theory. An awareness, decisions are not linear or simple, but the interdependence of agents influences what we decide to do.

Behavioural economics

The most important trend in recent decades in economics is the greater emphasis placed on aspects of behavioural economics, which uses many insights from related fields such as psychology.

•Disputes rational choice theory. The essential element of behavioural economics is that it argues individual agents are often not rational and often do not seek to maximise utility.

•Behavioural economics examines how agents can be influenced by biases, and make decisions not predicted by neo-classical economic theory. Behavioural economics can explain the irrational exuberance of booms and busts.

Econometrics

In the post-war period, economics became increasingly mathematical with economists attempting to use mathematics to explain models and theories. Econometrics looks at economic data and seeks to extract simple relationships. The basic tool is the linear regression models and can be used to try and predict consumer spending and demand for labour.

Heterodox models of microeconomics

Heterodox models differ substantially from microeconomic foundations of neo-classical economics. Schools of thought include

Marxist economic theory

Karl Marx developed an alternative perspective on economics. He focused on the surplus value created under the capitalist economic system. To Marx, the invisible hand of the market would be better described as the invisible hand of capitalist exploitation of workers. Marx claimed workers did receive their full labour value but were compensated for their necessary labour only – enabling capitalists to profit from the surplus.

Institutional economics. The role of society and institutions in shaping economic behaviour. For example, Thomas Veblen looked at theories of 'conspicuous consumption' and noted how the desire for social status could drive much economic theory. Institutional economics could be seen as a forerunner for later behavioural economics.

Environmental economics Argues traditional economics wrongly places value on increasing output. The most important thing is creating a sustainable environment which maximises living standards. So, manufacturers need to consider how to manufacture their products , but pollution can not be raised as the same time, because human will face to raise cost of living and living experiences to be poor , even food shortage, water pollution , air pollution , death rate raises when technological productivities brings pollution to our natural environment. Hence, environmental economoic theory is the most suitable to solve manufacturers' pollution problem.

Buddhist economics/non-profit goals. Like environmental economics, this questions the assumption higher incomes and higher output are desirable. The theory of hedonistic relativism suggests higher incomes do nothing to increase happiness levels, and traditional economics can encourage society to pursue materialistic goals which actually create more problems of stress, conflict and environmental degradation.

Some of the basic models you might find in A-Level economics :

•Price Discrimination

•Perfect competition

•Price Mechanism

•Monopoly

•Oligopoly and kinked demand curve

•Game Theory Pricing strategies

•Market failure

•Behavioural economics

ON conclusion, any macro economy theories can be applied to find the most reasonable methods to solve any customer problems in societies by economists as above. So, I believe that any economic and customer and social problems can be solved by economic theories in our society.

Demand and supply theory solves social problems

Over the past 20 years, many researchers believe to apply behavioral economic macroeconomic models which can predict market behavioral change. The reasons are based on assumptions of optimizing behavior in many cases have difficulty accounting for key real-world observations. Hence, researchers have used behavioral economics assumptions with the aim of making their model predicting better fit the data. The reason for behavioral economics results into macroeconomics will be more accurate to predict market behavioral change in macro-economy view point, such as economic fluctuation prediction, the consumption, formation of expectations and determination of wages and employment how to aggregation supply and the possibility of consumer individual demand product or service number prediction more accurately.

● How to apply behavioral economy (demand and supply) theory to predict marketing behavioral changes more accurate?

Anyway, economists aim to develop models of human behavior and interactions in market in order to build useful models. Economists make simplifying assumptions to analyze why the market will be changed by consumer individual consumption behavior changing.

Why do I assume consumers are as economic man ? In behavioral economy view point, how the perception of the economic man's behavior (including consumer choices) of economic models with the development of economics as a science. Economists explain the concept of economics as a science. It is the concept of consumer as an economic man, the essence and complexity of consumer behavior.

The consumer and consumer purchasing behavior are an important area of interest of many scientific disciplines. The process of economic decision making as well as consumption choices are connected with wider human activities. The terms of both consumer individual attitudes and group social behavior will influence group social behavior will influence consumer individual final consumption decision in every consumption choice process. Thus, behavioral economy method can predict consumer behavioral changing, it can apply these sciences to research, includes sociology, psychology, anthropology, operational research, decision theory etc. different literature research aspects. I assume that businessmen can apply behavioral economy method to predict market changing behaviors successfully if they own behavioral economy knowledge.

In this part, I shall concentrate on explain how the perception of the economic man's behavior (including consumer choice) is applied to predict market behaviors. After explaining the concept of consumer as an economic man, the nature and complexity of consumer behavior are discussed to below different industries' marketing behavioral changing every case studies in US or UK countries.

Why is consumer as an economic man in technological product market? IN behavioral economy view point, the concept of answer is one of the fundamental concepts in economics because the consumer is the case market participant along with the producer. In general, lecturers define the consumer in various ways, but in behavioral economy view point, consumers mean economy man. Because who will compare cost and benefit to any product or service to decide to choose to buy the product or consume the service. Consumers are as "economic man", who will make own subjective preferences (tastes), habits and traditions and existing objective constraints (i.e. disposal income) market prices of products and services in order to satisfy whose needs to a maximum degree and in the most rational way.

Thus, economic man means consumers need to make psychological mind to decide whether who either prefer to buy this product or another product or prefer to consume this service or another service more suitable. Thus, any markets or industries need have themselves benefits and consumers must need to evaluate whether the product or service has more benefits to compare other products or services in the consumption market to satisfy whose needs. It means that if the product or service has more benefits to compare other similar products or services. Then the product or service will persuade many consumers to choose to but the product or consume the service.

Consequently, in first part, I shall indicate how to apply behavioral economy theory : economic man psychological method, benefits and costs benefits method, how to predict these US and UK enterprises marketing behavioral changing more accurate.
In the second part, I shall apply micro employee behavioral economy concept to explain how to solve these US and UK inter-organizational management challenge.

I believe that behavioral economy method can be applied to research organizational employee behaviors change, e.g. how any why the employee chooses to do this action in whose organization. Moreover, behavioral economy method can be applied to consumption market to predict how any why the consumer choose to buy the product or consume the service. So, any consumers and employees personal psychology and external environment economic factor will influence how to choose to do decision in any organizations or consumption environment.

Bibliography

Bandiera, O., I. Barankay, and I. Rasul (2005). Social preferences and the response to incentives: Evidence from personal data. The quarterly journal of economics 120 (3), 917-969.

Exadaktylos, F., A.M. Espin and P. Branas-Garza (2013). Experimental subjects are not different. Scientific reports 3, 1213.

Lazear, E.P. (1979). Why is there mandatory retirement? Journal of political economy 87(6), 1261-1284.

● Behavioral economic method (demand and supply theory) predicts stable basic income consumer individual spending behavior to high technological product

Can apply behavioral economic method to predict that the consequences of a stable basic income consumer's consumption behavior in high technological product? It may be significantly different than the ones are predicted by the standard economic model if more realistic assumptions of human consumption behavioral prediction success.

Behavioral economic method assumes that consumer will compare whether whose benefits are more than costs after they buy the product or consume the service. I assume the consumer is only the who have stable basic income source consumer target. This stable basic income target consumers who will evaluate or feel they will earn more benefits than costs to every product in their consumption process, after they will make final decision to choose to buy the product to use or consume the service. Otherwise, if they feel they won't earn more benefits after they buy the product or consume the service in the consumption process. Then, they won't choose to buy the product to use or consume the service. In behavioral economic view point, it indicates their consumption behaviors are depend on comparing the product or the service whether it can satisfy their desire benefits and their desire benefits to the product or service must be more than their consumption cost.

There are four points to apply behavioral economic method to predict each stable basic income individual income spending. They include: motivation, conspicuous consumption, social preferences and crowding theory.

Each stable basic income consumer individual spending amount will be different and it is represent that every high stable basic income consumer must decide to consume any high cost services or buy high cost products to use. Although some economic teachers assume general high income people will accept to spend more expenditures for enjoyment or buy high cost of products to satisfy basic high level necessary expenditures. But, applying behavioral economic analysis, it is not absolute true, some low income people also accept to spend more to buy high cost of products or increasing spending expenditures for enjoyment for their basic necessary expenditures.

The field of behavioral economic can be fined as a combination of economics and psychology that tries to capture human behavior in a more realistic. Understanding each consumer individual consumption behavior, we need to know how who does each decision to influence each consumption choice. Consequently, analysis reaches the conclusion. Every high or low level stable basic income consumer individual behavioral consumption that the microeconomic consequences of a stable basic income of individual consumer target consumption group could be efficiency enhancing, but at the same time incentives about positional concerns could lead to wasteful and inefficient spending to the stable low basic income consumer target group.

● How to apply demand and supply theory to contribute to the stable basic income target consumer group's consumption prediction in high technological product market?

What is basic income mean? A basic income is an income paid by a political community to all its members on an individual basis, without means test or work requirement. How to apply behavioral economic method to contribute to the basic income consumption prediction?

I assume high income tax is charged to one high income tax payee , it will influence the high income tax payee individual consumption desires to be fallen, also extrinsic incentives will effort and intrinsic motivation and how the labor market change these variables under and big changes predicting, how income security changes social consumption preferences, e.g. how a big change affects the overall level of status -seeking behavior and this effect with income inequality to influence consumer individual consumption attitude or habit.

How can behavioral economic methods predict high technological product consumer's consumption decision, in special the stable basic income consumer target group? In any consumption decisions are involving risk and uncertainty, the standard economic model usually assumes that decisions are based on final condition, regardless of the changes are caused by the results of a consumer's decision.

An alterative mode of how consumers make decision and judgement under risk and uncertainty. This situation is often occurred in consumption market.

In behavioral economic view point, it explains how consumer's consumption, however, which excludes the stable basic income earn factor can influence the stable basic income earn target consumer group decides to make final consumption decision to compare to the non-stable basic income earn target consumer group. The reasons include as below:

(1) Consumers evaluate decisions over gains and losses with respect to some natural reference point, when they feel need to consume, which

is assumed to be judgement about a sequence of outcomes are based on changes in wealth, rather than whether how much absolute basic income earn to influence whose consumption desires.

(2) Thus, behavioral economic theory assumes the consumer is the low level of income group in society, but when who feels that he is still gains more than losses when who decides to buy the expensive product or consumes the expensive service. Then, the low level of income consumer who will accept to buy the expensive product or consume the service easily. Due to whose gains feeling is more than losses feeling, when who buys the product or consumes the service.

(3) Behavioral economic theory also assumes the taxpayer will pay high income tax in this year. The, even the high income taxpayer can earn high basic income, but due to whom needs to pay high income tax in this year. Then, he/she will reduce much spending, even he/she reduces spending on cheap products or cheap service consumption for enjoyment. This is the taxpayer's economic decision to influence whose consumption behavior, due to the high income tax expenditure factor influences whose consumption behavior to change to be reduced spending expenditures in this year.

How to apply behavioral economic method to encourage labor productivity in high technological product manufacturing industry?

Instead of applying behavioral economic method to predict every consumer individual consumption effort. Behavioral economic method can be also be applied to predict every country's labor market changing behavior. Particularly, how salary clerical workers or low wage labor workers should move from one type of job to another based on these factors. They include as below:

Their intrinsic motivation and how their levels of effort would change after this movement, investigates the effects of income security on social preferences in labor market changing behavior, and how cooperation in social contribution is affected when income security is guaranteed, how to predict the role of positional externalities on conspicuous consumption and how would change the incentive to influence consumption. So, it seems that general labor market job changing behaviors will not influenced by external economic environment better or worse changing factor, or salary changing factor etc. different environmental condition changing factors influence to employees' job changing. Generally, employee's job changing behavior is more influenced to persuade who changes job by himself/herself intrinsic motivation negative emotion influence mainly.

How to apply motivation crowding theory to predict labor productivity in high technological product manufacturing industry? One of the main challenges of economic theory is to find what are the optimal incentives that increase productivity of labors. The standing point is usually extrinsic incentive be it is form of monetary compensations for high effort or fine for low effort.

It is a kind method of reward or punishment to increase or decrease number of productivity to every labor. But it can only raise short term number of productivity in possible and it can not guarantee high quality of productivity. So if one employer wants a labor to do more of an activity or with a higher quality, consider paying the labor for working hard on punishing whom if for providing a low level effort.

This idea is that people do not like to work, and therefore they used some sort of compensation for doing a specific activity, and that the more they are paid the harder, they will work. So, payment better compensation is only beneficial to encourage labors to do one specific task or activity in short term. This method can not be suitable to rise long term beneficial productivity and high level quality of production or excellent performance in long term and it can only keep in short term raising productivity and high level quality of production or excellent performance benefits.

Consider paying the labor for working hard on punishing whom if for providing a low level effort. This idea is that people do not like to work, and therefore they used some sort of compensation for doing a specific activity, and that the more they are paid the harder they will work. So, payment better compensation is only beneficial to encourage labors to do one specific task or activity in short term. This method can not be suitable to raise long them beneficial productivity and high quality of products.

However, economists would argue that, is a labor has high intrinsic motivative to perform a task, who will provide a high level of effort without compensation by himself/herself but an even higher level of effort of whom is compensated. If a labor does not have any intrinsic motivation to perform a task or an activity, who will provide no effort or a low effort of whom. There is no compensation, but who will increase this level of effort of an extrinsic incentive is implemented.

Hence, in behavioral economic view point, the labor individual high level effort is a main psychological factor to influence whose productivity to be raised or the qualities of products to be raised, when the products are manufactured by the high level effort labor. It means that high compensation is not the good method to encourage labor productivity or raise quality. Otherwise, how to influence the one low level of effort of labor to change to be one high level of effort labor. It is the best psychological method to influence the labor to raise productivity and quality and service performance to any products or services in manufacturing process or service process for any organizations in long term beneficial possible.

● How can apply demand and supply theory raises basic stable income consumer high technological product purchase desire

Economists aim to develop models of human behavior and interactions in consumption markets. But consumers behave in complex ways, such as how to predict consumers to make rational decisions in consumption processes. Moreover, self-consumption control and motivation can vary significantly across different individual consumer.

In order to build useful consumption prediction models, economists make simplifying assumptions, aims to predict how to raise stable basic income consumer target group consumption more success. However, behavioral economy method is one kind of accurate consumption prediction method. It can be applied to predict economic decision-making to every consumer consumption choice more accurate raising whose consumption desire?

I shall indicate how to apply different behavioral economy methods (demand and supply theory) to raise stable basic stable income target consumer group consumption desire in these different consumption situation (consumption environment) aspects as below:

1. Stable basic stable income consumer group consumption great or small amount desire

The consumption of products and services is a fundamental part of consumer's welfare. Basically, every one who has stable basic stable income, who will like to consume any products and services. Even, consumption great or small amount desire won't be depended on whether the person whose income is more or less. It means low income level of people will still like to consume great amount to buy expensive products or consume expensive services, because consumption is human's part of life and basic needs.

This stable basic income people will like to consume, because they have stable income source when they do not worry about unemployment occurrence to cause them have no enough money to support their life. Otherwise, non-stable basic stable income people won't like to consume because they feel they have no stable basic income source to support their life and they will worry about unemployment occurrence any time. Hence, stable basic income people will have more consumption desire to compare non-stable basic stable income people in any countries usually. Behavioral economic method indicates they feel their economic benefits will be loss if they planned to buy any products or consume any services easily. So, they prefer to save money in bank more than consumption.

1. Demand systems and micro-economic factor influence basic income people high technological product purchase attitude

Why stable basic income people will like to consume? Because who have more demand, a demand system shows the level of consumer demand for different products and services: e.g. one basic stable income person may refer to the demand for clothes, another the demand for food etc.

How the demand for that particular product varies with the prices and demographic factor will influence who to accept consumption. Such as stable basic income people who will not consider to decide to buy the cloth to wear or the food to eat if who feel the cloth or food price is even more expensive to compare other kind of cloth or food.

Otherwise, non-stable basic income people who will consider to decide to buy the cloth to wear or the food to eat if they feel that they still have enough cloths to wear or enough food to eat at homes , even these food or cloth price are less expensive to compare others. Because they feel they lack stable income effort to support them to consume. Hence, basic stable income factor can influence the consumer's consumption decision.

2. Life-cycle advertisement method can influence consumer individual using high technological product time to be increased

Consumer behavior makes strong assumptions about the informational and computational bases of consumer behavior. Generally, consumer behavior is reasonably characterized as the maximization of expected lifetime utility subject to budget constraint and conditional on the available information.

Generally, consumers prefer to buy any discounted products or it is reasonable that consumers accept to buy many attractions to persuade them to buy any kinds of bargain discount products. Hence, low bargain discount product is one good behavioral economic principle to encourage or persuade or attract any consumers to increase consumption.

What is behavioral life-cycle model? This model explains consumer behavior can be persuaded to buy any discounted products by advertisement, e.g. television, radio, newspapers, magazine etc. promotion channels. Because frequent advertisement promotion method can let any consumers often remember the product's brand, discounted price, style, color and image from advertisement content.

So, advertisement can be one part of consumer behavioral life-cycle. For example, when the television audiences often watch TV. Hence, when the brand of product advertisement often makes fun image and discounted message to let TV audiences to remember this brand of product, when they are watching TV. Then, it has possible to persuade any potential consumers to choose to buy this brand of any products or consume this brand of any services, due to its advertisement of discounted sale message is very attractive to every one to let this advertisement audience's attention to remember this brand of products or services are selling or serving in market at this moment. So, it is advertisement image behavior influences audiences to buy the brand's any products attractively and persuasively.

3. Raising electricity consumption from electricity user individual habit can influence high technological products using time at homes ?

For electricity use market case example, how to analyze people's behavior in consuming electricity using a behavioral economic framework when householders need to use electricity to use their technological products, e.g. computer, television at homes ? Electricity consumption is modeled by the means of consumer's individual useful habit, electricity price, consumer satisfaction level, willingness to invest in new technologies, social interactions, and marketing strategies by the power utility. Because electricity is necessary to every home or electric vehicle users needs or businessmen office etc. different needs every day.

Power companies supply electricity to a region's homes and industries. However, electricity needs modernization of power system companies expect to increase price. Due to competitive factor, such as other fuel resource choices, outdated kind of energy electricity supply, and renewable fuel energy source competition.

Hence, applying behavioral economic concept, I assume electricity consumers will compare to electricity and other kinds of energy choices to weigh up the costs and benefits of all alternatives, aiming to maximize their benefits, before making a decision to choose to use electricity for their house electricity demand or electric vehicle or shop or factory manufacturing etc. function of different aspects of electricity users.

For example, electricity business clients, they aim to reduce cost, such as energy expenditure, when they use any energy to manufacture their products in factories. If they feel electricity is expensive price to compare other kinds of energy power supply. When, they feel that they can not earn much beneficial advantages to use electricity to produce their products. Otherwise, if they feel other any kinds of energy supply can replace electricity to give more benefits to compare electricity energy. Then, many business electricity users will change to use other kinds of energies to consume to replace electricity power.

However, electricity can have competitive ability in electric vehicles market, if many drivers feel environment protection is more important to compare vehicles will be popular to be driven, due to many drivers don't want air pollution. They will like gas vehicles. Hence, the main attribute from the consumer side is one their habit electricity consumption behaviors, satisfaction level, energy efficient interaction with the power utility.

Consequently how to predict electricity consumer's demand. The important factor is how to let electricity users to feel power companies are changing a reasonable level to compare other similar energy supply products. When electricity users feel electricity which can bring more benefits to compare other kinds of energy products. Then, in energy supply market, if the demanding number of electricity consumers can increase more than other kinds of energy demanding number. Then, it is right time to raise electricity price to charge electricity consumers. Hence, how to persuade electricity consumers to feel that they can have more benefits to compare other kinds of energy products. It is the main successful factor to electricity power supply companies.

● Consumer confidence is as a predictor of consumption spending

Behavioral economists believe it has link between confidence and economic decisions to cause consumers to choose spending, if the consumer has confidence to believe the product is worth to use, then who will accept to buy the product to use.

Concentrated on the conceptualization of confidence and its role in mode in theories of consumption. It also concerns on whether the confidence indicators contain any information beyond economic fundamentals. The concern is whether confidence can be explained by current and past value of variables, such as income, unemployment, inflation or consumption or in other way.

Whether confidence measures have any statistical significance in predicting economic outcomes once information from the above variables is used. Economic variable factor will also influence consumer confidence to decide consumption spending, e.g. real consumption expenditures (income, wealth or interest rate).

Finally, it will identify under which circumstances confidence indicates can be a good predictor of household consumption. Hence, survey is one good measurement method to predict whether how much every household has confidence to spend to consume the brand of products to use. Why is survey a good confidence consumption measurement prediction to every household in every country?

The reasons include survey can gather every household consumption habit history data to evaluate whether every survey person has how much confidence to consume the brand of products. Which in most cases correspond to periods where there are large changes in household survey indicators, liking during financial crises or geopolitical tensions to measure or predict whether the country's future good or bad economic condition factor will influence every household consumption desire in the year.

This modelling approach assumes that there is a certain (unknown) in confidence index changes beyond which confidence starts impacting consumption behaviors. So, sample household surveys can show the contribution of confidence in explaining consumption expenditures increases when household survey indicators feature large changes. So that confidence indicators can have some increasing predictive power during the survey investigation period in the year.

Other view point, surveys have been concerned on whether the confidence indicators contain any information beyond economic fundaments. The concern is whether confidence can be explained by current and past values of variables, such as income, unemployment, inflation or consumption or the other way. Whether confidence measures have any statistical significance in predicting economic outcomes once information from different external variable factors to influence the survey household group.

What is confidence in consumption survey ?

Confidence in consumption. For example, to measure whether how much degree of strong inflation in the economy, such as recessions and recoveries will influence the country's household confident consumption in the year. The surveys consumers' questions usually concern on major expenditures and changes in the respondent's financial situation, focus on job availability and current business conditions etc. questions. It is then possible that about consumer confidence depending on the relative performance of the variables that may be more relevant balances, with respect to the factors that determine unemployment and other labor market related issues. It aims to investigate whether those any one of variable factors will influence consumers general loss confident consumption desire in this year.

What is a confidence indicator ?

A confidence indicator is considered as an explanatory variable for consumption together with standard variables used on predicting consumption expenditure. However, the natural real personal consumption expenditure is unexpected and unpredicted easily.

In conclusion, consumption expenditure depends the consumer individual confidence. If the consumer has much confidence to feel this year economic change will be better and he/she is easily to find job, then he/she will accept consumption easily in this year. It seems financial wealth and unemployment etc. economic factors will influence every household consumption desire. So, survey is one kind of good psychological consumption prediction method to predict consumption spending for any country in the year. I recommend manufacturers may choose to apply survey method to attempt to enquire sample survey people to gather data to predict whether what degree of consumption desire to them and find solution methods to solve low degree of consumption desire challenge.

How to apply behavioral economy methods to influence employee individual psychology to achieve raise productivity of long term incentive intention?

Increasing salary is short term incentive productivity method. Behavioral economy assumes labors will choose to do beneficial behaviors to themselves when they feel their work behaviors can earn more benefits to themselves more than their employers in the organizations. Otherwise, if they feel their work behaviors can earn more benefits to their employers more than themselves. Then, they won't choose to do their work behaviors, e.g. raising productivities or work hard. Due to they feel work hard or raise productivities behaviors that only give more benefits to their employers more themselves.

Whether does cheap product price incentive consumption desire to influence effective consumption behavior? Whether is monetary increasing salary payment incentive labors might be willing to work on task? I feel raising labors productivities is similar to raise incentive consumption, which both have similar point, such as increasing salary payment or cheap product price is the main factor to influence incentive consumption or raising productivities. Hence, it seems monetary factor is not the main effort to encourage labors to work hard.

In labor's behavioral economic view point, for example, if an employer pays an employee more doing a task, who might be less willing to work on it, who might be less productive given whose efforts and who may enjoy the task less. If you want your employees to save more for retirement. You may want to give them fewer investment options. If you want them to engage more in a task, you might want offer them an additional alternative, instead of increasing salary to that task. Thus, increasing salary is not only method to encourage productivities of incentives.

How to improve the design of incentive structures to encourage productivities in any organizations?

Any monetary incentive can only encourage productivities in short term. It can not only encourage productivities in long term in any organizations. It is similar to cheap or discount product price can only attractive consumers to buy the product in short term, it can not attract consumers to choose to buy the product in long term, it prefers to have more options to encourage labors to incentive productivities, e.g. investing good beneficial retirement plans. Suggesting that employees do not have free disposal of their investment options. These standard incentives seem irrelevant raising salary monetary factor, they can be quite effective in inducing labors to take particular actions to incentive productivities in long term. Due to when they can hard work, then they have more beneficial retirement plans or investing plans for their retirement. It means when they can achieve the most effective or efficient productivities to the employer for long term. It will give better retirement benefits and investment benefits to the better or even the best performance of employees. Otherwise, the worst performance employees won't earn good retirement benefits and investment benefits, when their employers feel their perform very poor in the organizations in long term.

Hence, increasing salary level method is not one successful long term incentive method to persuade every employee to raise productivities or encourage excellent performance optional method. Increasing salary level is only similar to reduce product price and it is only short term encouragement to consumption or productivities method.

In conclusion, extrinsic monetary factor can not incentive labor's raising productivities more than every employee themselves intrinsic motivation to raise productivities as excellent performance in any organizations. Thus, organizations need to let employees to feel that they can give long term economic benefits to encourage their intrinsic motivation effort to be raised their productivities or performance more effective or efficient in order to achieve long term both win-win economic benefits to employees and employers both.

Can bonus method encourage high technological product workers productivities to be raised ?

In service job nature of bonus method can also raise employees' overall productivities or service performance. For example, when employees got a provisional bonus before the start of the workweek, but were warned that they would lose it on payday, unless they achieve the productivities or excellent service performance norm, they worked more productivities or let many clients to satisfy their service performance. Hence, managers can achieve bonus plan to compensate any excellent productivity or excellent services to them. Then, they can let clients to feel their service performance more satisfactory than employees of a control group who were merely given the standard promise to receive a bonus upon achieving the norm.

The effort was relatively small, however, productivity grew 1%. Interestingly, the effect of a loss was stronger when how teams were rewarded this way, social pressure came to bear on the less productivity team members. When the team members won't earn any bonus. So, long-term productivity gains were achieved through bonuses paid by excellent performance compensation method to compare to low service performance employees receiving no bonuses at all.

Economic views of human motivation nature

There are only two main types of economic actors and by making simplifying assumptions about how these types of actors behave and interact. The two basic sets of actors in this model are firms, which are assumed in this model are firms, which are assumed to maximize their profits from producing and selling products and services, households, which are assumed to maximize their utility (or satisfaction) from consuming products and services.

It seems any employees will choose to do behaviors to achieve to earn much benefits from their organizations. The models of economic behaviors that consider considerate employees' choice of goals, the actions they take to achieve these goals and the limitations and influences that affect their choices and actions.

For university students choose which universities to study case, suppose that any college enrollment students are deciding which courses to study. Thus, it implies that if the university can provide many different kinds of suitable or right courses to any college enrollment students to choose to study. It means that if the university can provide many different kinds of courses to enrollment students to choose to study. Then, it will have much chance to attract enrollment students to choose this university to study. It's competition can be raised by many courses choice factor. but, in fact, it is not absolute right, although the university can provide many courses to provide to enrollment students to choose to study. But, it is not guarantee to represent it must attract many students to enroll this university to study.

For example, suppose that college enrollment students are deciding which courses to choose to study. Although, it has right course to prepare to these enrollment students to choose to study. But, they see a summary of evaluations from hundreds of other students indicating that a certain course is very good in this university. Then, suppose that they match a video interview of just one student to give a negative review of this university of the course. Even when students were told in advance that such a negative review was worse to this university of the course. They tended to be more influenced by the negative review than the summary of hundreds of evaluations, even although such behavior seems irrational. Hence, although many right courses choice has much chance to attract students to enroll this university to study. But, if its bad educational quality from this course from negative review factor, which will influence the enrollment students number to be reduced.

It implies that students will compare this university's the course educational quality whether is better or worse to compare other universities' similar course educational quality, even this university's this course fee whether is reasonable in educational market. This is cost and beneficial comparison behavioral economy principle to all enrollment students before they decide to choose which universities.

Hence, this case implies that universities how to train teachers' teaching skills to let students to feel that they can learn new knowledge from their teaching staffs absolutely. It means how to raise education training skills to raise teachers' teaching performance. It is very important factor to influence the university's teaching development success. So, many courses choice is not important factor to attract many students to enroll the university. Otherwise, although the university can not provide many courses to let students to enroll, but it's teachers can provide excellent teaching service to teach whose students. This is important factor to attract many students to choose to enroll this university to study.

Under-level productive efficiency and low-consumption desire behavioral economic influences high technological products demand and supply and price raises or reduces relationship

In behavioral economic influence view point, I feel that under-level productive efficiency is the represent low production number to the manufacturer as well as low-consumption desire is not represent less consumers demands or customers lose confidence to the product.

On the one hand, I shall apply behavioral economic method to analyze why under productive efficiency is not represent low production number influence. Otherwise, I feel under-productive efficiency will have possible to increase production number after the manufacturer can review what factor(s) to influence under-productive efficiency.

I shall give reasons to explain as below:

As Jim, P. & Brendan. M. (2013) indicated who had ever been experiencing failure to do their businesses. Although, they had lost a million dollars, but they felt that they can be taught to learn undiscovered knowledge to know how to do their businesses successful by their wrong judgement and decision learning experience. They explained that " in ll risk taking, speculation, business ventures, entrepreneurial activities, it is the loss side on which you must focus first. This is even true for gambling, the gambler determines how much he's willing to bet, and loss, before the game is played. He doesn't wait for the game to end and then let the croupier or dealer assign his wager for him. How do you determine the downside, and how do you control or minimize it? With objective decision making and a plan that has as its starting point the stop-loss parameters"

Hence, it explains any business will have under-level productive efficiencies and low consumption desire business risk. However, to any one entrepreneur, who needs to know it is one game between the himself/ herself and whose clients. They also need to know with objective decision making and a plan that has as its starting point.

Hence, I assume that if the entrepreneur has wrong decision to cause under-level productive efficiency, it is possible that, due to there is no enough employee number to manufacture the product or many employees are not skillful to manufacture all product in normal time or many employees are lazy etc. different factors to cause under-level productivities. However, when they discover their productivities are very low to compare similar competitors their employees' productivities and efficiencies. Then, they can attempt to find what factor(s) to cause low productivities and low efficiencies. it is possible that any one among of these factors case. They include many employees' lazy to influence low productivities or there is no enough employee number or many employees are not skillful to manufacture their products in production process.

Hence, wrong decision or plan is not represent failure. Otherwise, it can give chance to let the entrepreneur to learn whether what the factor(s) is (are) to cause low productivities and low efficiencies in whose product manufacturing process. As I feel that under-level productive efficiency is not represent low production number. Because I assume that if one worker lacks enough skills and manufacturing experiences to manufacture the product, but who can spend less time to manufacture the product and whose spending manufacturing time is same to the another owning enough skillful worker's time to do the product. Hence, I believe that the product quality from the low-skillful worker's manufacturing skill, it's quality will be worse to compare to the product quality from the high skillful worker's manufacturing skill. Hence, if the low skillful worker needs to spend much time to produce the product, but the product quality can be same to the high skillful worker's product quality. It means that it is sure because the low skillful worker has no excellent skill to compare to the high skillful worker to produce the product. Hence, his manufacturing spending time must be longer than the high skillful worker's time. It implies that the low skillful worker spends less time to raises high production number, but his product must be poor quality to sell. Then, his fast and efficient manufacturing speed that is not achieve economic beneficial to the organization's manufacturing process, e.g. less electricity spends to manufacture the product. Otherwise, the low skillful worker's fast and efficient manufacturing speed of behavior will raise the organization's cost in manufacturing process because consumers would not like to choose to buy any low quality product when they can choose which similar products to compare which one has the best quality and cheap price to buy.

Hence, efficient production is not the main factor to influence the business's success. Otherwise, good quality of the product factor is more important to compare it to influence the business's success.

On the other hand, I shall apply behavioral economic theory to analyze why low-consumption desire is not represent consumer demand lose to the business. As Jim. P. & Brendan. M. (2013) also identified " rather than looking for success to follow, who explained the formula for failure to avoid. As an Wang, founder of Wang laboratories said " it is my belief that there are no secret to success." The formula for failure is not lack of knowledge, brains, skills or hard work and it's not lack of luck, it's personalizing losses, especially of preceded by a string of wins or profits. It's refusing to acknowledge and accept the reality of a loss when it starts to occur because to so so would reflect negatively on you."

Thus, as whose feeling to explain why low-consumption desire is not represent less consumers demands or customers lose confidence to the product. The reasons include the causes of low-consumption desire are possible due to worse economic environment factor influences consumption desire to be reduced. It is not due to whether the product price is too high or quality is worse to compare others. Hence, as Jim & Brendan indicated the formula for business failure is not lack of knowledge, brains, skills or hard work and it's not lack of luck. It's not lack of luck. It's personalizing losses, means its reflecting to knowledge and accept the reality of a loss when it starts to occur. As it is applied to explain why low-consumption desire is not represent less consumers demands or customers lose confidence to the product. It's possible that external economic environment changing worse factor to cause the business personalizing losses, it is not reflect who lacks knowledge, skill, hard work factors to cause failure. Hence, ho to predict when and how and why economic environment changes worse will be important factor to predict when and how and why consumption behavioral changes to cause business's success.

● Demand and supply theory solves high technological product salespeople performance problems

Any high technological product sale organizations, e.g. computer shop, washing machine or mobile or televison shops can let salespeople feel happy to sell their products. Then their sale performance will also raise. The question concerns that how to make them to feel happy to help the organization to sell their products? I shall explain some methods as below:

How to manage sales for predictable revenue? In order to hold salespeople sale psychology whether they feel happy or unhappy, executives need to understand the essential activities, sales managers must focus on to be analysts for change, foster continuous improvement and create a sales culture that drives results. Sale executives need to know how to achieve top objectives of sales management is to drive sales, capture new revenue and exceed monthly sales and margin objectives, e.g. performing sale straregy development with each salesperson on Monday morning at a minimum, and in a formal one-on-one meeting during the week;using strategy tools and questioning techniques to ensure the prospects are qualified and the strategy is valid; knowing the ratio between future values and future monthly quotos to raise sale opportunities; six month on-going sale plan aims to make sure there are coordinated to achieve sale to various market segments; developing on ongoing series of networking events to build market awareness in order to ensure all salespeople attend specific events involved in networking by salespeople to, understanding the market how to influence salespeople sale method to sale number, understanding trends and seeking some channels to raise additional sales opportunities; how to create trained or warm sale environment to let sales teams feel happy to sell.

How to design and utilize efficient control sale procedures? The sale cycle procedure may include these market activities, such as advertising, sales promotion, market research, physical distribution, pricing , sale place, sale staffs seeking. SO, any organizations need have good sale planning, direction and control of the personnel, selling activities of a business with including recruiting, selecting, training, rating, supervising, paying or reward system, motivating strategy , as all these tasks apply to the personnel sales-force.

The factors may influence salespeople psychology, they may include fair income reward system, or appreciation methods and sale career development plan to every salesperson. It aims to encourage them to achieve the highest sale effort. Anymore, methods to train sale managers have the right direction to guide, lead and motivate their salespeople, e.g. knowledge of salespeople psychology needs how to satisfy them, understanding why they choose to do or act themselves sale behaviors in order to improve their weakness to motivate salespeople to achieve company's sale target goal every month easily, e.g. raising profitability, sales volume, market share, growth and corporate image building raise clients' confidence to choose to buy this company's any products more easily.

The sales organization is required for the following purposes, they may include: enabling top-management, to devote to more time in policy making for the growth and expansion of business to divide and fix authority among the subordinates , so that they may shirk work, to avoid repetition of duties and functions, so that there may not be any confusion among them to locate responsibility of each and every employee , so that they can complete the whole work in stipulated time, if not then the particular person must be responsible, to establish the sales effort to enforce proper supervision of sales force.

What does the concept of salespeople replacement value mean? What is a sales force turnover management tool? Sales force turnover is defined as the rate at which salespeople leave an organizations, resignations, retirements or dismissals. So, if the organization can raise the sales force turnover ratio, because many salespeople can be promoted or the retirement, or the sales force turnover ratio raising reasons as well as they are not resignation or dismissal reasons. I believe that the organization ought have good sale environment and reasonable reward and welfare strategy to let its salespeople feel happy to help this company to sell its products every day.

However, sales management's actions have direct or indirect effects to impact on turnover. Direct effects may include the firm's firing or dismiss policy. The indirect effects on sale turnover may include new salesperon recruiting and selecting policies affect the quality and performance of the sale force as well as the speed at which salespeople are replaced. The same policies have an impact on the sales force turnover rate through the characteristics of the newly recurited salespersons and the promotion , training, retraining policies, support, supervision, compensation. ALl of those factors have an impact on salesperson's personal satisfaction or dissatisfaction absolutely. So, any sale organizations need to concern how and why whether any one of above these factors may influence their salespeople how to perform or act sale behaviors in order to excite their sale number more effective in long term.

How to achieve sale force management effectively? Sale management is one strategy to many organizations, because organizations expect their salespeople can only raise product sale number. So , they will consider whetther how to implement the sale management strategy to be the most suitable to themselves sale organizations in order to excite their sale teams to sell their products to achieve sale growth aim effectively. So for organization's long term sale growth development, it seems that one excellent sale management strategy can help the organization has stable sale number growth in long term possible.

However, the term " selling" includes a variety of sales situations and activities. For example, those sales positions where the sales representative is required primarily to deliver the product to the customer on a regular or periodic basis. The emphasis is this type of sales activity is very different to the sales position where the sales representative is dealing with sales of capital equipment to industrial purchasers. IN additions some sales representatives deal only in export markets whereas others sell direct to customers in their homes. So, sale organizations need to sell to local or overseas market as well as its target customer is businessmen or individual consumer or both in order to implement to choose their most suitable sale management strategy to train their salespeople more effective or achieving sale growth objective only. Because these its sale major target and where sale market place both factors will influence how it ought train its salespeople, so any organization's training method ought be influenced to change by whom is its major sale target and where is its major sale market location factors.

How to know the psychology of salesmanship? WHen the organization can predict or find reasons to explain why its salespeople feel unhappy to help
this organization to sell its products. Then, it can attempt to improve its weaknesses in order to let its salespeople to feel more sale service satisfactory feeling to continue to help this organization to sell its products. THen, it won't need not often to train or recruit new salespeople to replace its old salespeople in consequence. How to know what its salespeoples' real need in order to raise their sale service satisfactory feeling ?

Psychology means that " science of the mind" and psychology plays to important part in business and it is quite worth to bring to influence any organization salespeoples' posivitive or negative sale emotion in their every sale process between themselves and their every client in personal. For example, if the salesperson often have negative emotion or he feels unhappy in every sale process, then he will encounter or increase many times of sale failure possibilities. He will feel that he is one poor verbal advertiser or seller or promotor to help his organization to promote its products to sell again as well as he will lose confidence to sell any products next sale chance, because his failure sale experiences are accumulated to influence his sale emotion to be poor or difficult sale.

Hence, the poor performance salesperson needs have more successful sale experiences to compensate his / her prior many sale failure times feeling, if the organization hopes this poor performance salesperson can raise sale number easily. Overall, any organizations need to concern how to improve or raise the more failure times of sale experience salespeoples' sale techniques or methods or attitudes more than choose to fire or dismiss them as well as finding another new salesperson to replace him/her. Because it is possible that the salesperson 's poor sale performance that is not due to himself/herself poor sale effort and sale knowledge or lacking sale experience to the product, it may be due to the poor sale team cooperation relationship , feeling poor or not comfortable sale physcial shop environment, poor sale manager and other salespeople working relationship, the sale manager lacks leadership effort, poor family relationship etc. external factors more than himself/herself personal poor or negative emotion or poor health etc. personal factors. Hence, the organization ought enquire him/her why he/she feels unhappy to sell its products and it needs to attempt to find methods to solve his/her challenges immediately. If his/her challenges can be solved. It is possible that his/her sale efforts can be also raised for. So, if the organization can know how to utilize positive sale emotion psychological methods to predict or know why and how every salesperson perform his/her sale behavior in whose daily sale tasks, then it can concentrate on implementing effective and the most suitable sale training to raise their sale abilities more easily.

However, the sale training may include: How to build or improve long term good salesperson and his/her customer sale service relationship between every salesperson and every client in every buying and selling cycle process, how to using right communicating styleds for better understanding every client's real needs, powers and negotiating, e.g. every salesperson needs to review why there are many clients do not choose to buy any products from his sale presentation or promotion, finding every time sale failure reasons can let the salesperson makes himself/herself sale failure reasons evaluation or judgement in order to find what is the major reason influences his/her sale failure, e.g. lacking product knowledge, he/ she often let many clients to feel that he lacks patience to listen the client's enquiry or feedback, his sale presentation is not attractive to let many clients like to stay longer time to listen his sale presentation in whole sale process, the salesperson himself/herself emotion is negative and he /she can let many clients feel he / she is not happy or does not enjoy to sell this product from himself/herself face impression or sale behavior impression easily, lacking enough sale techniques to persuade his/her clients why he/she ought choose to buy this product in whole sale process etc. these factors may influence the salesperson's sale failure chance to be raised. Hence sales manager ought need to spend long time to meet the poor sale performance salesperson to discuess what his/her sale challenges are the most major to influence his/her every sale successful chance in order to improve his/ her sale performance more successfully.

IN conclusion, the reasons why salespeople often encounter sale failure possibilities. The factors may include these aspects, such as they lask the desire to help customers to make satisfactory purchase decisons, they only concern how to achieve sale final objective or aim only, it will cause clients feel they do not real concern their real needs. They only concern to sell the product in success. They do not know how to describe the product whether what characteristics or features it owns accurately in order to increase sale chance to persudade them to make final decision to by the product, they do not attempt to participate the whole sale process to help them to choose the most right product in order to satisfy their any purcahse needs, they ought avoid deceptive or manipulative influence tactics, avoid the use of high pressure sales techniques etc. Thus, if any organizations can spend time to investigate what factors cause why any one of salespeople choose perform his/her sale behavior often in order to know or understand their salespeople' sale psychology absolutely. Then, I believe that their sale number will only grown more easily.

CHAPTER THREE

Information Society factor raises high technological product needs

What does information society mean? Why can information society influence high techhological products needs increase ? Information Society is a term for a society in which the creation, distribution, and manipulation of information has become the most significant economic and cultural activity. An Information (knowledge) Society may be contrasted with societies in which the economic underpinning is primarily Industrial . The machine tools of the Information Society are computers and telecommunications, rather than lathes or ploughs. An information society is a society where the creation, distribution, use, integration and manipulation of information is a significant economic, political, and cultural activity. Its main drivers are digital information and communication technologies, which have resulted in an information explosion and are profoundly changing all aspects of social organization, including the economy, education, health, warfare, government and democracy. The people who have the means to partake in this form of society are sometimes called digital citizens. Those who use the Internet regularly and effectively". This is one of many dozen labels that have been identified to suggest that humans are entering a new phase of society.

Webster, Frank (2002) explained that the markers of this rapid change may be technological, economic, occupational, spatial, cultural, or some combination of all of these .Information society is seen as the successor to industrial society. Closely related concepts are the post-industrial society, post-modern society, knowledge society, Information Revolution, network society.

There is currently no universally accepted concept of what exactly can be termed information society and what shall rather not so be termed.
Most theoreticians agree that a transformation can be seen that started somewhere between the 1970s and today and is changing the way societies work fundamentally. Information technology goes beyond the internet, and there are discussions about how big the influence of specific media or specific modes of production really is. Frank Webster notes five major types of information that can be used to define information society: technological, economic, occupational, spatial and cultural. According to Webster, the character of information has transformed the way that we live today. How we conduct ourselves centers around theoretical knowledge and information.

How much degree has social media changed our societal high technological products needs increase?

The question made why me think about how much has changed in society (whether we realize it or not) as a result of social media to influence high technological products needs raise. Think about it, it was only approximately 20 some odd years ago that the average person was beginning to become associated with the internet. Prior to that, the internet was mostly reserved for academia and various government agencies.

Before that it was only reserved for the U.S. government (the official origins of the internet began back in 1969 with the U.S. military's funding of a research network dubbed "Arpanet").Today, we have not only the internet, but we have social media tied in there as well. As the term "social media" implies: "media" is a place where publications occur. "social" implies that there is sharing occurring. A sharing of ideas, opinions, images.

The social in social media also implies the tools, places and services that allow people to gather for social interaction. Social media allows individuals to gather and express themselves in a much more simple and immediate fashion. By giving people this capability, they not only have the ability to share ideas, opinions and other contents, but also (if they wish) gain notoriety, and expand their influence.

What are benefits of using Social media for high technological products Businesses ?

The ability to do so has altered the way ideas change hands and how fast those ideas spread. At the same time, news and
any information that would usually take days or even weeks to go from one

location to another can now occur in seconds. This ease of communication has never been so available to people around the world as it is now and it is still continuing to evolve. Remember that throughout history, many countless numbers of governments have created and held onto their power by controlling information and the spreading of ideas. Because of social media, many of these types of governments can no longer function this way any longer.

Because the technology available to a person is so economical and simple to utilize that virtually anyone with some education or training on the subject can become a point of contact for the communication of information.

The Delivery of News, the Sharing of Ideas, the Expression of Opinions .The spreading of an idea, or of news occurring somewhere in the world can no longer be completely blocked by any organization. As long as one person is able to connect to the internet and express their view about a situation or simply about an idea, then the information that individual will want to share, will get out into the world.

Remember, last year during the Iranian elections when there were (and to some extent still are) people disagreeing with the "official" election outcome, the Iranian government attempted to control the communication and the images of what was occurring in Iran from getting out. They were never able to control all the information and images that were being seen by the world in 'real-time'. In another example, when an earthquake rocked the country of Haiti, not only were images from the torn country in the aftermath of the quake being seen around the world but commentaries and opinions of what people were seeing were being read and heard (from Haiti).

Sites such as Facebook, Twitter, YouTube allow people to share ideas on not just news, but also on products and services. Products and Services that before social media, many people would not have even heard about them, let alone request or want the service. Needless to say, social media has forever changed the way society works, whether it's the sharing of an idea, the communication of news, or the availability of a product or service. Society today is on the verge of a new way of existing that it's never experienced before. No longer will people from one side of the world be really able to say that they will never see a person or communicate with someone from the other side of the world ever in their life. No longer will people not be able to share an idea, if they really want to share it (no matter how radical it may be or no matter how many people may disagree with it). No longer will the spreading of information or the expressing of an opinion be able to be completely silenced.

As long as there is a person who wishes to express their opinion, share their music or art, or simply say hello to another human being in another country or culture, social media will allow them to do so.

· What are some of your opinions as to how social media has changed society?

· How do you believe social media will be in the future?

· What will social media look like 15 or 20 years from now?

Do we live in a change or in a changing society to influence our needs to improvement of high technological products needs raise? How can one characterize the deep transformations that come with the accelerated insertion of artificial intelligence and new Information and Communication Technologies (ICTs) in our present society?

Is it a question of a new stage in the industrial society or are we entering into a new social change? "Global village", "post-industrial society", "information society" or "information age", and "knowledge society" are just a few of the terms that have been coined in an attempt to identify and understand the extent of these changes. But while the debate proceeds in the theoretical sphere, reality races ahead and communication media select the terms that we are to use.

The bottom line is: whichever term we use, it will be a shortcut that allows us to reference a phenomenon - be that present or future -, without having to repeatedly describe it; however, the selected term in itself does not define content. Content emerges from usage within a specific social context, which in turn influences perceptions and expectations, since each term brings with it a past and a meaning (or meanings), with its respective ideological baggage. It was therefore to be expected that any term used to designate the society in which we live, or to which

we aspire, be the focal point of a dispute over meanings, backed by the varied opposing projects of society.

Within the benchmark of the World Summit other Information Society (WSIS) there are two terms that have occupied the scenario: information society and knowledge society, with their respective variants. But, although the benchmark imposed usage of the former, from the beginning it caused disagreement and no single term has achieved a consensus.

Why can information society influence high technological products demands raise?

In this past decade, the expression "information society" has without a doubt been confirmed, not because it necessarily expresses a theoretical clarity, but rather due to its "baptism" by the official policies of the more developed countries and the "crowning" that meant having a World Summit dedicated in its honor. In 1973, United States sociologist Daniel Bell introduced the notion "information society" in his book The Coming of Post-Industrial Society , where he formulates that the main axis of this society will be theoretical knowledge and warns that knowledge-based services will be transformed into the central structure of the new economy and of an information-led society, where ideologies will end up being superfluous.

This expression reappears strongly in the 90s, within the context of the development of the World Wide Web and ICTs. As of 1995, it was included in the agenda of the G7 meetings (followed by G8, which joins heads of State and governments from the most powerful nations on the planet). It has been addressed in forums of the European Community and the OECD - Organization for Economic Cooperation and Development (the thirty most developed countries in the World), and has been adopted by the United States government, as well as various UN agencies and the World Bank Group. All with great repercussions in the communication media. As of 1998, the term was first selected by the International Telecommunication Union (ITU) and then by the UN, as the name for the World Summit to be held in 2003 and 2005.

Within this context, the concept "information society" as a political and ideological construct has developed under the direction of neo-liberal globalization, whose main goal has been to accelerate the establishment of an open and "self-regulated" world market.
This policy has counted on the close collaboration of multilateral organizations such as the World Trade Organization (WTO), the International Monetary Fund (IMF), and the World Bank, in order for the weak countries to abandon national regulations or protectionist measures that "would discourage" the inversion; all with the known result of a scandalous widening of the gaps between the rich and the poor in the World.

In fact, at the end of the century, when the majority of the developed countries had already adopted ICT infrastructure development policies, there is a spectacular peak in the share market of the communications industry. But the markets in the North begin to become saturated. Then, increased pressure is placed on the developing countries to leave the way free for investments by telecommunications and informatics companies, in search of new markets to maintain growth of earnings. However, when the stock bubble burst as of the year 2000. Regardless of this reality and the key role that communication technologies have played in the acceleration of economic globalization, information society's public image is more associated with the "friendlier" aspects of globalization, such as the World Wide Web, mobile and international phoning, TV via satellite, etc. Thus, the information society has assumed the role of the "good will ambassador" for globalization, whose "benefits" could be within the reach of all, if only the "digital divide" could be bridged.

What can knowledge society influence high technological products needs raise?

The notion "knowledge society" emerged toward the end of the 90s and is particularly used as an alternative by some in academic circles to the "information society".in particular, has adopted the term "knowledge society", or its variant, "knowledge societies", within its institutional policies. There has been a great deal of reflection on the issue, which strives to incorporate a more integral conception that is not only related to the economic dimension.

For example, Abdul Waheed Khan (general sub-director of UNESCO for ? Communication and Information) writes : "Information society is the building block for knowledge societies. Whereas I see the concept of 'information society' as linked to the idea of 'technological innovation', the concept of 'knowledge societies' includes a dimension of social, cultural, economical, political and institutional transformation, and a more pluralistic and developmental perspective.

In my view, the concept of 'knowledge societies' is preferable to that of the 'information society' because it better captures the complexity and dynamism of the changes taking place. (...) the knowledge in question is important not only for economic growth but also for empowering and developing all sectors of society." In this debate, which only concerns the distinction between that "knowledge society" be translated as the "intelligence society". It is necessary to differentiate here between those definitions that aim to characterize an existing or emerging reality from those that express a vision-a longing or desire- for a potential society. Both are relevant: the former for their contribution to analysis, and the latter because they guide policies and actions.

In the first category, we will refer the term "informational society" to "information society" (making the comparison with the difference between industry and industrial). He points out that while knowledge and information are decisive elements in all modes of development, "the term informational indicates the attribute of a specific form of social organization in which information generation, processing, and transmission are transformed into the fundamental sources of productivity and power, due to the new technological conditions that arise during this historic period."

Further on, we need to ask this question:

What characterizes the current technological revolution is not the central personage of knowledge and information, but rather the application of this knowledge and information to knowledge generation and information/communication processing devices, in a cumulative feedback loop between innovation and the uses of innovation?

As for the knowledge society, in a later publication of some authors, they have different views, they indicate: "it has to do with a society in which the conditions for generating knowledge and processing information have been substantially changed by a technological revolution focused on information processing, knowledge generation, and information technologies." "information society" places the emphasis on the content of the work (the process of collecting, processing, and communicating the necessary information), and "knowledge society" emphasizes economic agents, who should be superiorly qualified to exercise their work.

In fact, the entire process had been crossed by (at least) two separate approaches, which can be briefly summarized as follows:

In the first approach, to talk about the information society refers to a new business and economic development that assigns technology to a causal role in the social order, designating it as the drive of economic development. For the developing countries, this discourse implies that the transition towards the information society is essentially a matter of time and of political decision to create adequate "empowering conditions". Something similar occurred with regard to the social sectors affected by the digital gap, which would have to be included via universal access programs. By placing technology at the core of this model, the telecommunications industry is convoked to lead this development.

The second approach, information society means the new phase of human development that we are entering into is characterized by the predominance of information, communication, and knowledge in the economy as well as human activities. According to this standpoint, technology is the support that has unleashed the acceleration of this process; but it is not a neutral factor, nor is its course inexorable, since technological development is guided by games of interest.

Following this perspective, policies for information society development should focus on human beings and should be conceived in terms of their needs and within a benchmark of human rights and social justice. The developing countries and the social actors should play a key role in the orientation of that process and the decisions.

In other words, for this second approach, what is fundamental is not "information" but rather "society". While the first approach refers to data, transmission channels, and storage space, the second talks about human beings, cultures, forms of organization and communication. The information is determined in terms of society and not the inverse. That is why the campaign for Communication Rights in the Information Society -CRIS- points out "The Question for Civil Society" "If civil society is going to adopt and recover the notion of an information society, it should return to these basic notions, posing the correct questions:

- Who generates and possesses information and knowledge? How is it valued?

- How is knowledge spread and distributed? Who are the custodians?

- What restricts and facilitates the use of knowledge on the part of people to attain their goals? Who is best and least positioned to take advantage of this knowledge?"

However, given the predominance acquired by the term "information society", alternative formulations tend to use this term as a demarcation reference. An initial objection has to do with the word "society" in the singular, as if it was dealing with a uniform world society. The proposed alternative is to speak about information or knowledge "societies" (using plural). Several UNESCO documents refer to "knowledge societies". And in fact, civil society consensus documents adopted the formula "information and communication societies" in order to be set apart from the techno-centric vision. One could consider that this option was an important gesture within the context of the WSIS; but it does not escape from being a weighty formulation for current usage.

As for the debate on the "knowledge society", those who uphold it consider that it evokes precisely a more integral vision and an essentially human process. Others, however, object to it for its association with the dominant concept that reduces knowledge to its economic function (the notion, for example, of "knowledge management" in companies, which emphasizes essentially how to assert one's claim to and take advantage of employees' knowledge);
which values only the type of knowledge that is supposedly objective, scientific, and digitizable,that which is not.

So an information society needs to be important to understand what this concept covers: it does not have to do with information that is disseminated and shared, but rather with a society in which there is a wish to communicate in another manner and share knowledge. It has to do then with a shared knowledge society and a knowledge society."

In conclusion, we can explain that the concept "information society", born under the precepts of neo-liberal globalization, infers that henceforth it will be the "technological revolutions" that will determine the course of development; social conflicts would be things of the past. For the same reason, this concept is no longer the most appropriate to qualify the new trends in societies. Our position is that, beyond debating the appropriateness of one term or another, what is fundamental is to contest and delegitimize any term or definition that reinforces this techno-centric conception of society. Lastly, we are backing a project of society where information is a public good, not a commodity; communication, a participative and interactive process; knowledge, a shared social construction, not private property; and technologies, a support for it all, without becoming an end in itself.

CHAPTER FOUR

What are information society influences to high technological products market

What is information technology and moral values relationship to influence high technological products needs ?

Every action we take leaves a trail of information that could, in principle, be recorded and stored for future use. For instance, one might use the older forms of information technologies of pen and paper and keep a detailed diary listing all the things one did and thought during the day. It might be a daunting task to record all this information this way but there are a growing list of technologies and software applications that can help us collect all manner of data, which in principle, and in practice, can be aggregated together for use in building a data profile about you, a digital diary with millions of entries. Some examples of which might be: a detailed listing of all of your economic transactions; a GPS generated plot of where you traveled; a list of all the web addresses you visited and the details of each search you initiated online; a listing of all your vital signs such as blood pressure and heart rate; all of your dietary intakes for the day; and any other kind of data that can be measured. As you go through this thought experiment you begin to see the complex trail of data that you generate each and every day and how that same data might be efficiently collected and stored though the use of information technologies.

It is here we can begin to see how information technology can impact moral values. As this data gathering becomes more automated and ever-

present, we must ask who is in control of collecting this data and what is done with it once it has been collected and stored? Which bits of
information should be made public, which held private, and which should be allowed to become the property of third parties like corporations? Questions of the production, access, and control of information will be at the heart of moral challenges surrounding the use of information technology.

One might argue that the situation just described is no different from the moral issues revolving around the production, access, and control of any basic necessity of life. If one party has the privilege of the exclusive production, access, and/or control of some natural resource, then that by necessity prohibits others from using this resource without the consent of the exclusive owner. This is not necessarily so with digital information. Digital means that we can all, at least theoretically, possess the same digital information without excluding its use from others. This is because copying digital information from one source to another does not require eliminating the previous copy. Unlike a physical object, theoretically, we can all possess the same digital object as it can be copied indefinitely with no loss of fidelity. Since making these copies is often so cheap that it is almost without cost, there is no technical obstacle to the spread of all information as long as there are people willing to copy it and distribute it. Only appeals to morality, or economic justice might prevent the distribution of certain forms of information. For example, digital entertainment media, such as songs or video, has been a recurring battleground as users and producers of the digital media fight to
either curtail or extend the free distribution of this material

How information technology influences our mass media on social relationship ?

In the last five decades or so, the media and its influence on the societies, has grown exponentially with the advance of technology. First there was the telegraph and the post offices, then the radio, the newspaper, magazines, television and now the internet and the new media including laptop or desktop , cell phones , radio etc. There are positive and negative influences of mass media, which we must understand as a responsible person of a society.
Before discussing the influence of mass media on society it is imperative to explain the three basic functions of mass media; they are providing

news/information, entertainment and education. The first and foremost function of the media in a society is to provide news and information to the masses, that is why the present media change is some time termed as the information age as well.

People need news/information for various reasons, on one hand it can be used to socialize and on the other to make decisions and formulate opinions. Entertainment would be the other function of the mass media where it is mostly used by the masses to amuse them in present day environment. Educating the masses about their rights, moral, social and religious obligations is another important function of mass media, which needs no emphasis.In present globalization, majority of people in the society depends on information and communication to remain connected with the world and do our daily activities like work, entertainment, health care, education, socialization, travelling and anything else that we have to do.

A common urban person usually wakes up in the morning checks the TV news or newspaper, goes to work, makes a few phone calls, eats with their family or peers when possible and makes his decisions based on the information that he has either from their co workers, TV news, friends, family, financial reports, etc. we need to be conscious of the reality that most of our decisions, beliefs and values are based on what we know for a fact, our assumptions and our own experience. In our work we usually know what we have to do, based on our experience and studies, however on our routine life and house hold chores we mostly rely on the mass media to get the current news and facts about what is important and what we should be aware of.

We have put our trust on the media as an authority to give us news, entertainment and education. However, the influence of mass media on our kids, teenagers and society is so big that we should know how it really works. The media makes billions of dollars with the advertising they sell and that we are exposed to, every single moment. We buy what we are told to buy by the media. After seeing thousands of advertising's we make our buying decisions based on what we saw on tv, newspapers or magazines. These are the effects of mass media especially in teenagers, they buy what they see on TV, what their favorite celebrity advertise and what is acceptable by society based on the fashion that the media has imposed on them.

There are some positive and negative influences in young people of our society due to these ad campaigns in the media. Here is a positive influence example, if there is a quiz show on education that is getting a lot of attention by the media and gains popularity among your friends and society, you will more likely want to actively participate and watch these quiz shows. These activities are good for the society and will promote literary activities in the youth. However a negative influence in teenagers is the use of guns and ammunition by celebrity movie stars, the constant exposure of which would seduce the teen to replicate the same behavior in the real life.

When we watch TV or an action movie we usually see many images of violence and people hurting others. The problem with this is that it can become traumatic especially in our children as they see it more and more. Our kids that are starting to grow and are shaping their personality values and beliefs can become aggressive or they can lose a sense of distinction between reality and fiction. Another problem is that real war is used as a form of entertainment by the media, we should make our kids and teen aware that war is not a form of entertainment and that there is no win or lose like in video games, in real war everyone lose. Teens, youngsters are in a stage of life where they want to be accepted by their peers, they want to be loved and be successful.

The media creates the ideal image of beautiful men and women with all the ingredients of a successful person, you can see it in movies and TV. It's a subliminal way to persuade the masses that if you want to be successful and look like them then you have to buy that particular brand or product. Another negative influence in teenagers, especially in the USA, that has grown over the last years is obesity. There are millions of adolescents fighting obesity, but at the same time they are exposed to thousands of advertisements of junk food, while the ideal image of a successful person is told to be thin and wealthy.

The media has a huge impact on society in shaping the public opinion of the masses. They can form or modify the public opinion in different ways depending of what is the objective. Before that the public opinion over the military action against the Taliban in Swat was divided, but repeated telecast of this short video clip changed the public opinion over night in the favor of the government to take action. Other ways to influence are with polls and trends, especially in political campaigns. The candidates that can pay for more TV and media exposure have more influence on public opinion and thus can receive more votes.

How information technology impacts our Society and Its Future to high technological products market ?

As we are aware of Information Technology had its modern existence from late sixties of the last century when the Arpanet was introduced, funded by the department of defense of USA. After that the IT industry has come a long way to its current shape where it is playing a very dominant role in our every sphere of life. It has made revolutionary changes in information gathering and dissemination as well as in global communication. It is creating a virtually paperless work environment. Also we can now send a message very easily to anywhere in the world in seconds. From education point of view we can have a virtual class where the instructor could sit in any part of the world and his students scattered in all different parts of the world through video conference with presentation of study materials as well as question and answer sessions. A doctor now sitting in any part of the world could perform a surgery where the patient is lying in another part of the world. These simple examples show where we stand today compared to what it was half a century back. But as we know nothing in this world is purely good as everything has a dark side. In this paper we would discuss the merits and demerits of implementing IT globally and where we are heading to in future.

The first definition is of "information technology". Information technology is the technology used to store, manipulate, distribute or create information. The type of information or data is not important to this definition. The technology is any mechanism capable of processing this data. As it is widely known to perform a calculation of any type manually is very cumbersome and time consuming. But if we could develop efficient programs written in many languages and get them thoroughly tested for every function it is expected to perform before putting to use could save lot of efforts and time. Also the chance of human errors that could occur when things are done manually could also be avoided provided the programs are developed keeping in mind the exact requirements that are sought after and developed properly to address the issues correctly without problems. Information technology works based on these simple concepts. As we know it's applications in our lives is extremely wide ranging from simple addition, subtraction to flying an aircraft though autopilot and controlling a spaceship which has landed in Mars from the ground of the earth. Electronic databases now can store huge volume of data which can be used very easily and internet can be accessed for any information on any field of activities.

The influence of information technology on religious practices has mainly been to the effect of making information about them more accessible. The most relevant question though is whether the developments in information technologies have influenced the continuity of social attitudes, customs or institutions. Social attitudes have changed with the effect that citizens of a society now expect the various elements of that society to be better informed than previously. They also expect to be able to access more information about a specific product, service or organization so that they can make informed decisions with regard to their interactions with that entity. The "government" of a nation will be comprised of many varied institutions.

However developments in information technology have helped governments to improve their "service" to their citizens. Advances in Database technology for example have enabled the governments of various countries to collate and monitor statistical information that they can use to combat fraud and manage the economy in a more informed way. Information Technology also has a major impact on the defense capabilities of governments. This covers both a government's capability to wage war and their intelligence gathering capability. Advances in weapons technology and weapons design have increased the effectiveness of various governments' armed forces. Information Technology has also had a major impact on a government's

intelligence agencies. Encryption of sensitive information has enabled governments to obtain added security. However attempting to decrypt information is also a major area of work for those employed by the government. The advances in information technology have heavily influenced commercial businesses in several ways. The most important role of information technology in a commercial business, however, is to provide a commercial advantage. Advances such as computer aided design, relational database technologies, spreadsheets, and word processing software all provide a commercial benefit to the business, as does automation of manufacturing processes. The use of information technology to monitor a business performance can also enable the business to highlight areas where they are not making the most use of their resources. The use of information technologies can also increase the businesses income through advertising in the various available forums. Developments such as the Internet and satellite television have created new media and audiences through which and to which News & Media organizations can disseminate their information .An infrastructure of computing and communication technology, providing 24-hour access at low cost to almost any kind of price and product information desired by buyers, will reduce the information barriers to efficient market operation. This infrastructure might also provide the means for effecting real-time transactions and make intermediaries such as sales clerks, stock brokers and travel agents, whose function is to provide an essential information link between buyers and sellers redundant.

The information technologies have facilitated the evolution of enhanced mail order retailing, in which goods can be ordered quickly by using telephones or computer networks and then dispatched by suppliers through integrated transport companies that rely extensively on computers and communication technologies to control their operations. The impact of information technology on the firms' cost structure can be best illustrated on the electronic commerce example. The key areas of cost reduction when carrying out a sale via electronic commerce rather than in a traditional store involve physical establishment, order placement and execution, customer support, staffing, inventory carrying, and distribution. Although setting up and maintaining an e-commerce web site might be expensive, it is certainly less expensive to maintain such a storefront than a physical one because it is always open, can be accessed by millions around the globe, and has few variable costs, so that it can scale up to meet the demand. By maintaining one 'store' instead of several, duplicate inventory costs are eliminated.

Computers and communication technologies allow individuals to communicate with one another in ways complementary to traditional face-to-face, telephonic, and written modes.
They enable collaborative work involving distributed communities of actors who seldom, if ever, meet physically. These technologies utilize communication infrastructures that are
both global and always up, thus enabling 24-hour activity and asynchronous as well as synchronous interactions among individuals, groups, and organizations. By reducing the fixed cost of employment, widespread telecommuting should make it easier for individuals to work on flexible schedules, to work part time, to share jobs, or to hold two or more jobs simultaneously. Since changing employers would not necessarily require changing one's place of residence, telecommuting should increase job

mobility and speed career advancement.

This increased flexibility might also reduce job stress and increase job satisfaction .The rapid increase in computing and communications power has raised considerable concern
about privacy both in the public and private sector. Decreases in the cost of data storage and information processing make it likely that it will become practicable for both government and private data-mining enterprises to collect detailed dossiers on all citizens. Nobody knows who currently collects data about individuals, how this data is used and shared or how this data might be misused. These concerns lower the consumers' trust in online institutions and communication and, thus, inhibit the development of electronic commerce.

A technological approach to protecting privacy might by cryptography although it might be claimed that cryptography presents a serious barrier to criminal investigations.

It is popular wisdom that people today suffer information overload. A lot of the information available on the Internet is incomplete and even incorrect. People spend more and more of their time absorbing irrelevant information just because it is available and they think they should know about it. Therefore, it must be studied how people assign credibility to the information they collect in order to invent and develop new credibility systems to help consumers to manage the information overloads . Technological progress inevitably creates dependence on technology. Indeed the creation of vital infrastructure ensures dependence on that infrastructure.

As surely as the world is now dependent on its transport, telephone, and other infrastructures, it will be dependent on the emerging information infrastructure. Dependence on technology can bring risks. Failures in the technological infrastructure can cause the collapse of economic and social functionality. Blackouts of long-distance telephone service, credit data systems, electronic funds transfer systems, and other such vital communications and information processing services would undoubtedly cause widespread economic disruption. However, it is probably impossible to avoid technological dependence.

Therefore, what must be considered is the exposure brought from dependence on technologies with a recognizable probability of failure, no workable substitute at hand, and high costs as a result of failure .Increasing representation of a wide variety of content in digital form results in easier and cheaper duplication and distribution of information. This has a mixed effect on the provision of content. On the one hand, content can be distributed at a lower unit cost. On the other hand, distribution of content outside of channels that respect intellectual property rights can reduce the incentives of creators and distributors to produce and make content available in the first place. Information technology raises a host of questions about intellectual property protection and new tools and regulations have to be developed in order to solve this problem. There are a lot of positive things to do with social communication for example you can communicate with people at the other end of the world there is no limit to how far you can communicate as long as there is another person who is able to reply to your email / Facebook comments. You can meet a lot more friends over the social network and can arrange to meet new people. The internet is a wonderful thing when it comes to searching for information. People who would like to learn new things can do this via the internet you don't need to read paragraphs and paragraphs of information you can just get the answer you need by a click of a mouse. Improved communication using email, social networking - This is a good way to communicate. People use the web to send emails to people at other ends of the world. They do this because it is a cheap and easy and quick way to communicate .This is a bad thing because you do not know who you are talking to and if you arrange to meet this person they might not be who you think they are and this is a big danger and can hurt people a lot .

Cyber stalking- This is quite possibly one of the worst things that happens on the internet. These things happen every day and can lead to all sorts of things like people hurting other people, people threaten other people or even people getting depressed because of it and going and hurting themselves. More information available - This is one great thing about the internet that you can find all the information in the world on it. This can help you in all your work. You can find out anything what is going on. Quicker access to information for coursework- The internet is a great place to research information for the topic that you are doing. You can find all sorts of facts and opinions in seconds. Investments to increase the level of explicit coordination with outside agents have generally resulted in increased risk to the firm; firms have traditionally avoided this increased risk by becoming vertically integrated or by under investing in coordination.

Some economists argue that information technology (IT) has the ability to lower coordination cost without increasing the associated transactions risk, leading to more outsourcing and less vertically integrated firms, when our society encounters the information society stage to bring this reducing cost disadvantage to firms or businessmen. Lower relationship-specificity of IT investments and a better monitoring capability imply that firms can more safely invest in information technology for inter firm coordination than in traditional investments for explicit coordination such as co-located facilities or specialized human resources; firms are therefore more likely to coordinate with suppliers without requiring ownership to reduce their risk. This enables them to benefit from production economies of large specialized suppliers.

Moreover, rapid reduction in the cost of IT and reduction in the transactions risk of explicit coordination makes possible substantially more use of explicit coordination with suppliers. The resulting transaction economies of scale, learning curve effects, and other factors favor a move toward long-term relationships with a smaller set of suppliers. The society in the developed countries will be divided into two major groups: On the one hand, there will be technophile people, who embrace the new Possibilities which Information Technology offers to their lives. On the other hand, there will be technophobic people, who will obstruct the inroads of Information Technology into their daily lives. Contrary to what most people would think, this part of the population will not only consist of ecologists, but also of conservative people who see technology as something unnatural for humanity, people who don't immediately profit from technological progress such as the rural population and people who are simply overwhelmed by the new technologies and cannot keep up with the pace anymore. This group of technophobic people has a potential to grow temporarily to at most 25% of the total population. The definition of society for the 75% of the population who will embrace Information Technology will change radically.

What makes a society today will not be of much importance in the future? People would these days agree that a society is defined mostly by location, language, culture, political system, shared customs, standard of living and common history. Most of these things will fade in importance, instead other things will be much more important, namely personal preferences and interests. Due to the new technical possibilities, societies will look different and consist of different kind of people. POSITIVE IMPACTS OF ICT ON PEOPLE Access to information: Possibly the greatest effect of ICT on individuals is the huge increase in access to information and services that has accompanied the growth of the Internet.

Some of the positive aspects of this increased access are better, and often cheaper, communications, such as VoIP phone and Instant Messaging. In addition, the use of ICT to access information has brought new opportunities for leisure and entertainment, the facility to make contacts and form relationships with people around the world, and the ability to obtain goods and services from a wider range of suppliers. Improved access to education, e.g. distance learning and on-line tutorials. There are new ways of learning, e.g. interactive multi-media and virtual reality. There are new job opportunities, e.g. flexible and mobile working, virtual offices and jobs in the communications industry. New tools, new opportunities: The second big effect of ICT is that it gives access to new tools that did not previously exist.

A lot of these are tied into the access to information mentioned above, but there are many examples of stand-alone ICT systems as well: ICT can be used for processes that had previously been out of the reach of most individuals, e.g. photography, where digital cameras, photo-editing software and high quality printers have enabled people to produce results that would have previously required a photographic studio. ICT can be used to help people overcome disabilities e.g. screen magnification or screen reading software enabling partially sighted or blind people to work with ordinary text .NEGATIVE IMPACTS OF ICT ON PEOPLE Job loss: One of the largest negative effects of ICT can be the loss of a person's job. This has both economic consequences, loss of income, and social consequences, loss of status and self-esteem. Job losses may occur for several reasons, including: manual operations being replaced by automation e.g. robots replacing people on an assembly line. Job export. e.g. data processing works being sent to other countries where operating costs are lower. Multiple workers are being replaced by a smaller number who are able to do the same amount of work e.g. a worker on a supermarket checkout can serve more customers per hour if a bar-code scanner linked to a computer is used to detect goods instead of the worker having to enter the item and price manually. Reduced personal interaction: Being able to work from home is usually regarded as being a positive effect of using ICT, but there can be negative aspects as well. Most people need some form of social interaction in their daily lives and if they do not get the chance to meet and talk to other people he or she may feel isolated and unhappy. Reduced physical activity: A third negative effect of ICT is that user may adopt a more sedentary lifestyle.

This can lead to health problems such as obesity, heart disease, and diabetes. Many countries have workplace regulations to prevent problems such as repetitive strain injury or eyestrain, but lack of physical exercise is rarely addressed as a specific health hazard .ICT CAN HAVE A POSITIVE EFFECT ON ORGANIZATIONS By using ICT has brought a number of benefits to organizations, such as: Cost savings by using e.g. VoIP instead of normal telephone, email / messaging instead of post, video conferencing instead of traveling to meetings, e-commerce web sites instead of sales catalogues. This could allow access to larger, even worldwide markets .

With the development of computer industry and internet networks during the last three decades things have changed and global communication has reached an unprecedented height. With these developments immense scopes have come to the surface to impart learning in a much more efficient and interactive way. Multimedia technology and internet networks have revolutionized the whole philosophy of learning and distance learning and provided us with the opportunity for close interaction between teachers and learners with improved standard of learning materials compared to what was existing only with the printed media. As we mentioned earlier it has gone to such an extent to create a virtual class room where teachers and students are scattered all over the world. We could be able to work on jobs being thousands of miles away through electromagnetic wave. So, when we counter information society, teachers and students and online workers ought feel more convenient from internet learning media.

That way the problem of skills shortage in some countries could be reduced and efficient people would be available to do the job. Quick dispatch of information globally has facilitated the commercial expansion to an extremely high level with a small firm being able to sell its products to another part of the world very easily as they can communicate to each other in no time and fix up the deal. Development of electronic commerce has made it very convenient for individual buyer to select the product online and make payment immediately. However this has its problem as the buyer has not seen whom he/she is buying from and can never hear from the seller once the money has been paid. This kind of case has come to our attention. Virtual reality, probably much more advanced and more seamlessly integrated devices (e.g. one could think of a device projecting images (perhaps from glasses) directly onto the lens of a human's eye), allowing people to disregard their surroundings. This will allow people to travel virtually, e.g. one could go on holidays just by playing a certain program, relax there, walk around, take it easy. These days one can attend business meetings without having to be there physically. The business partners in such a virtual meeting are able to see and hear each other as if they are real. Mobility may be very important these days, however, in the new century, the need to travel physically is decreasing significantly, instead of flying to a meeting in New York one can just attend the meeting virtually and save a lot of time and money (and protect the environment).Contact with other people will only happen if desired by a person, everything else will be done by technology. As an example, nobody will need to go shopping anymore, one will order things needed via some special sophisticated devices which are easy to handle and understand. One can display the goods, possibly even smell, feel or hear them. Treating untreatable disease like cancer would be much easier as the DNA structure could be defined accurately to guide the kind of cell-based treatment required for a particular patient. So, information society can encourage consumers to apply internet to carry on any online shopping, when many customers accept online shopping method to replace traditional store shopping method. It is one technological innovation shopping experience to let consumers to feel. It means that future consumer behavior will be influenced to choose online shopping activities and online product information gathering method more than traditional TV, radio, magazine media product information gathering method. SO, it seems that it has cause and effect relationship between informational society and ecommerce. Hence, environment protection high technological products need will be rasied, when many people feel environment protection needs.

In conclusion, the impacts of information technology in our lives so far. It brings human the positive and negative effects of information technology, like loss of privacy, unauthorized access to important data. Hacking of government run systems by hackers can paralyze a government functioning and can cause immense disruptions. But we believe benefits from information technology far outweigh the negative aspects of information technology. As we discussed we can access information for our studies or research very quickly these days. Also the global communications have become unbelievably quick through email services. We strongly believe in future also information technology would bring much more conveniences in our lives than any negative impacts.

Information society can bring influences to impact our society as below several aspects, I shall indicate as below:

What are our nowadays information social business models, commerce and market structure ?

One important way in which information technology is a connecting work is by reducing the importance of distance. In many industries, the geographic distribution of work is changing significantly. For instance, some software have been found that they can overcome the tight local market for software engineers by sending projects to India or other nations where the wages

are much lower. Furthermore, such arrangements can take advantage of the time differences, so that critical projects can be worked on nearly around the clock. Firms can outsource their manufacturing to other nations and rely on telecommunications to keep marketing, R&D, and distribution teams in close contact with the manufacturing groups.

Thus the technology can enable a division of labor among countries, which in turn a connects the relative demand for various skills in each nation. The technology enables various types of work and employment to be decoupled from one another. Firms have greater freedom to locate their economic activities, creating greater competition among regions in infrastructure, labor, capital, and other resource markets. It also opens the door for regulatory, it can increasingly choose which tax authority and other regulations apply.

Computers and communication technologies also promote more market-like forms of production and distribution. An infrastructure of computing and communication technology, providing 24-hour access at low cost to almost any kind of price and product information desired by buyers, will reduce the informational barriers to client market operation. This infrastructure might also provide the means for connecting real-time transactions and make intermediaries such

as sales clerks, stock brokers and travel agents, whose function is to provide an essential information link between buyers and sellers, redundant. Removal of intermediaries would reduce

the costs in the production and distribution value chain. The information technologies have facilitated the evolution of enhanced mail order retailing, in which goods can be ordered quickly by using telephones or computer

networks and then dispatched by suppliers through integrated transport companies that rely extensively on computers and communication technologies to
control their operations. Nonphysical goods, such as software, can be shipped electronically, eliminating the entire transport channel. Payments can be done in new ways. The result is disintermediation throughout the distribution channel, with cost reduction, lower end-consumer
prices, and higher product margins.

The impact of information technology on the cost structure can be best illustrated the electronic commerce example. The key areas of cost reduction when carrying out a sale via electronic commerce rather than in a traditional store involve physical establishment, order placement and execution, customer support, inventory carrying, and distribution. Although setting up and maintaining an e-commerce web site might be expensive, it is certainly less expensive to maintain such a storefront than a physical one because it is always open, can be accessed by millions around the globe, and has few variable costs, so that it can scale up to meet the demand. By maintaining one 'store' instead of several, duplicate inventory costs are eliminated. In addition, e-commerce is very effective at reducing the costs of attracting new customers, because advertising is typically cheaper than for other media and more targeted.Moreover, the electronic interface allows e-commerce merchants to check that an order is internally consistent and that the order, receipt, and invoice match.

Through e-commerce, they are
able to move much of their customer support on line so that customers can access databases or manuals directly. This significantly cuts costs while generally improving the quality of service. E-commerce shops require far fewer, but high-skilled, employees. E-commerce also permits savings in inventory carrying costs. The faster the input can be ordered and delivered, theless the need for a large inventory. The impact on costs associated with decreased inventories is most pronounced in industries where the product has a limited shelf life (e.g. bananas), is subject to fast technological obsolescence or price declines (e.g. computers), or where there is a rapid expansion of new products (e.g. books, music). Although shipping costs can increase the cost of many products purchased via electronic commerce and add substantially to the significant price, distribution costs are significantly for digital products such as financial services, software, and travel, which are important e-commerce segments.

Although electronic commerce causes the disintermediation of some intermediaries, it creates greater dependency on others and also some entirely new intermediary functions. Among the intermediary services that could add costs to e-commerce transactions are advertising, secure
online payment, and delivery. The relative ease of becoming an e-commerce merchant and setting up stores results in such a huge number of offerings that consumers can easily be overwhelmed. This increases the importance of using advertising to establish a brand nameand thus generate consumer familiarity and trust.

For new e-commerce start-ups, this process can be expensive and represents a significant transaction cost. The openness, global reach, and lack of physical clues that are inherent characteristics of e-commerce also make it fraud and thus increase certain costs for e-commerce merchants as compared to traditional stores. New techniques are being developed to protect the use of credit cards in e-commerce transactions, but the need for greater security and user verification leads to increased costs. A key feature of e-commerce is the convenience of having purchases delivered directly. In the case of tangibles, such as books, this incurs delivery costs, which cause prices to rise in most cases, thereby negating many of the savings associated with e-commerce and substantially adding to transaction costs.

With the Internet, e-commerce is rapidly expanding into a fast-moving, open global market with an ever-increasing number of participants. The open and global nature of e-commerce is likely to increase market size and change market structure, both in terms of the number and size of players and the way in which players compete on international markets. Digitized products can cross the border in real time, consumers can shop 24 hours a day, seven days a week, and are increasingly faced with international online competition. The Internet is helping to enlarge existing markets by cutting through many of the distribution and marketing barriers that can prevent from gaining access to foreign markets. E-commerce lowers information and transaction costs for operating on overseas markets and provides a cheap consumption way
to strengthen customer-supplier relations. It also encourages companies to develop innovative ways of advertising, delivering and supporting their product and services. While e-commerce on the Internet is popular on the potential for global markets, certain factors, such as language, transport costs, local reputation, as well as
differences in the cost and ease of access to networks, attenuate this

potential to a greater or lesser extent.

(1) Information society impacts workplace and labor market aspect in high technological product manufacturing industry method

Computers and communication technologies allow individuals to communicate with one another
in ways complementary to traditional face-to-face, telephonic, and written modes. They enable collaborative work involving distributed communities of actors who seldom, if ever, meet physically. These technologies utilize communication infrastructures that are both global and always up, thus enabling 24-hour activity and asynchronous as well as synchronous interactions among individuals, groups, and organizations. Social interaction in organizations will be influenced by use of computers and communication technologies. Peer-to-peer relations across department lines will be enhanced through sharing of information and coordination of activities.
Interaction between superiors and subordinates will become more tense because of social control issues raised by the use of computerized monitoring systems, but on the other hand, these of e-mail will lower the barriers to communications across different status levels, resulting in more uninhibited communications between supervisor and subordinates.

That the importance of distance will be reduced by computers and communication technology also favors telecommuting, and thus, has implications for the residence patterns of the citizens. As workers that they can do most of their work at home rather than in a centralized workplace, the demand for homes in climatically and physically attractive regions would increase. The consequences of such a shift in employment from the suburbs to more remote areas would be profound. Property values would rise in the favored destinations and fall in the suburbs. Rural, historical, or charming aspects of life and the environment in the newly attractive areas would be threatened. Since most telecommuters would be among the better educated and higher paid, the demand in these areas for high-income and high-status services like gourmet restaurants and clothing boutiques would increase. Also would there be an expansion of services of all types, creating and expanding job opportunities for the local
population.

By reducing the cost of employment, widespread telecommuting should make it easier for individuals to work on schedules, to work part time, to share jobs, or to hold two or more jobs simultaneously. Since changing employers would not necessarily require changing one's place of residence, telecommuting should increase job mobility and speed career advancement. This increase might also reduce job stress and increase job satisfaction. Since job stress is a major factor governing health there may be additional benefits in the form of reduced health costs and mortality rates.

On the other hand one might also argue that technologies, by expanding the number of different tasks that are expected of workers and the array of skills needed to perform these tasks, might speed up work and increase the level of stress and time pressure on workers. A question that is more difficult to be answered is about the impacts that computers and communications might have on employment. The ability of computers and communications to perform routine tasks such as bookkeeping more rapidly than humans leads to concern that people will be replaced by computers and communications. The response to this argument is that even if computers and communications lead to the elimination of some workers, other jobs will be created, particularly for computer professionals, and that growth in output will increase overall employment. It is more likely that computers and communications will lead to changes in the types of workers needed for different occupations rather than to changes in total employment.

A number of industries are a connected by electronic commerce. The distribution sector is directly affected, as e-commerce is a way of supplying and delivering goods and services. Other industries, indirectly a connected, are those related to information and communication technology(the infrastructure that enables e-commerce), content-related industries (entertainment, software), transactions-related industries (financial sector, advertising, travel, transport). Ecommerce might also create new markets or extend market reach beyond traditional borders. Enlarging the market will have a positive effect on jobs. Another important issue relates to interlinkages among activities a

connected by e-commerce. Expenditure for e-commerce-related intermediate goods and services will create jobs indirectly, on the basis of the volume of electronic transactions and their effect on prices, costs and productivity. The convergence of media, telecommunication and computing technologies is creating a new integrated supply chain for the production and delivery of multimedia and information content. Most of the employment related to e-commerce encounters around the content industries and communication infrastructure such as the Internet.

Jobs are both created and destroyed by technology, trade, and organizational change. These processes also underlie changes in the skill composition of employment. Beyond the net employment gains or losses brought about by these factors, it is apparent that workers with different skill levels will be affected differently. E-commerce is certainly driving the demand for IT professionals but it also requires IT expertise to be coupled with strong business application skills, thereby generating demand for a flexible, multi-skilled work force. There is a growing need for increased integration of Internet front-end applications with enterprise operations, applications and back-end databases. Many of the IT skill requirements needed for Internet support can be met by low-paid IT workers who can deal with the organizational services needed for basic web page programming. However, wide area networks, competitive web sites, and complex network applications require much more skill than a platform-specific IT job. Since the skills required for e-commerce are rare and in high demand, e-commerce might accelerate the upskilling trend in many countries by requiring high-skilled computer scientists to replace low-skilled information clerks, cashiers and market salespersons.

(2) Information society impacts high technological products needs to education aspect

Advances in information technology will affect the craft of teaching by complementing rather than eliminating traditional classroom instruction. Indeed the effective instructor acts in a mixture of roles. In one role the instructor is a supplier of services to the students, who might be regarded as its customers. But the effective instructor occupies another role as well, as a supervisor of students, and plays a role in motivating, encouraging, evaluating, and developing students. For any topic there will always be a small percentage of students with the necessary background, motivation, and self-discipline to learn from self-paced workbooks or computer assisted instruction. For the majority of students, however, the presence of a live instructor will continue to be far more e-connective than a computer assisted counterpart in facilitating positive educational outcomes. The greatest potential for new information technology lies in improving the productivity of time spent outside the classroom. Making solutions to problem sets and assigned reading materials available on the Internet offers a lot of convenience. E-mail vastly simplify communication between students and faculty and among students who may be engaged in group projects.

Although distance learning has existed for some time, the Internet makes possible an large expansion in coverage and better delivery of instruction. Text can be combined with audio/ video, and students can interact in real time via e-mail and discussion groups. Such technical improvements coincide with a general demand for retraining and upskilling by those who, due to work and family demands, cannot attend traditional courses. Distance learning via the
Internet is likely to complement existing schools for children and university students, but it could have more of a substitution effect for continuing education program. For some degree program, high-prestige institutions could use their reputation to attract students who would otherwise attend a local facility. Owing to the Internet's ease of access and convenience for distance learning, overall demand for such program will probably expand, leading to growth in this segment of e-commerce.

As shown in the previous section, high level skills are vital in a technology-based and knowledge-intensive economy. Changes associated with rapid technological advances in industry have made continual upgrading of professional skills an economic necessity. The goal of lifelong learning can only be accomplished by reinforcing and adapting existing systems of learning, both in public and private sectors. The demand for education and training concerns the full range of modern technology. Information technologies are uniquely capable of providing ways to meet this demand. Online training via the Internet ranges from accessing self-study courses to complete electronic classrooms. These computer-based training program provide skills acquisition and are more affordable and relevant than more traditional seminars and courses.

(3) Information society impacts private life and society privacy aspect to high technological application

Increasing representation of a wide variety of content in digital form results in easier andcheaper duplication and distribution of information. This has a mixed e-connect on the provision of content. On the one hand, content can be distributed at a lower unit cost. On the other hand, distribution of content outside of channels that respect intellectual property rights can reduce the incentives of creators and distributors to produce and make content available in the first place. Information technology raises a host of questions about intellectual property protection and new tools and regulations have to be developed in order to solve this problem.

Many issues also surround free speech and regulation of content on the Internet, and there continue to be calls for mechanisms to control objectionable content. However it is very difficult to a sensible solution. Dealing with indecent material involves understanding not only the views on such topics but also their evolution over time. Furthermore, the same technology that allows for content altering with respect to decency can be used to alter political speech and to restrict access to political material. Thus, if censorship does not appear to be an option, a possible solution might be labeling. The idea is that consumers will be better informed in their decisions to avoid objectionable content.

The rapid increase in computing and communications power has raised considerable concern about privacy both in the public and private sector. Decreases in the cost of data storage and information processing make it likely that it will become practicable for both government and private data-mining enterprises to collect detailed dossiers on all citizens. Nobody knows who currently collects data about individuals, how this data is used and shared or how this data might be misused. These concerns lower the consumers' trust in online institutions and communication and, thus, inhibit the development of electronic commerce.

A technological approach to protecting privacy might by cryptography although it might be claimed that cryptography presents a serious barrier to criminal investigations. It is popular wisdom that many people today feel information overload. A lot of the information available on the Internet is incomplete and even incorrect. People spend more and more of their
time absorbing irrelevant information just because it is available and they think they should know about it. Therefore, it must be studied how people assign credibility to the information they collect in order to invent and develop new credibility systems to help consumers to manage the information overload.

Technological progress inevitably creates dependence on technology. Indeed the creation of vital infrastructure ensures dependence on that infrastructure. As surely as the world is now dependent on its transport, telephone, and other infrastructures, it will be dependent on the emerging information infrastructure. Dependence on technology can bring risks. Failures in the technological infrastructure can cause the collapse of economic and social functionality. Blackouts of long-distance telephone service, credit data systems, electronic funds transfer systems,and other such vital communications and information processing services would undoubtedly cause widespread economic disruption. However, it is probably impossible to avoid technological dependence. Therefore, what must be considered is the exposure brought from dependence on technologies with a recognizable probability of failure, no workable substitute at hand, and

high costs as a result of failure.

Does Information society influence our lives to be better?

I am inclined to favor the idea that technology does enrich our lives. It provides us with a huge quantity of information and entertainment.

For example, if you search something in the internet, you will see tons of information about it, and some of that you could not find otherwise. Even though our modern technology provides us with these sorts of amazing services, pessimists have a different perspective. Pessimists point out that technology is destroying our relationships and creating security threats, but can they state that technology affects our lives in a negative way just because it sometimes causes problems in our communities? No. All things and choices have some unpleasant consequences, and we just have to bear them. Also, they should consider about how technology can be very useful in weather forecasting, medical treatment, warfare, and et.

When the first three classes of needs are satisfied, the needs for esteem can become dominant. These involve needs for both self-esteem and for the esteem a person gets from others. Humans have a need for a stable, firmly based, high level of self-respect. and needs for Self-Actualization.

When all of the foregoing needs are satisfied, then and only then are the needs for self-actualization activated. Maslow describes self-actualization as a person's need to be and do that which the person was "born to do." Nowhere in Maslows Hierarchy of needs does it say that we need technology to live a happy and fulfilled life. Our lives being "better" as stated in the resolution rely on physiological needs, safety needs, needs of love and acceptance, needs for esteem, and needs for self actualization.

Technology cannot provide for any of these needs and is actually damaging to several of them. For example, technology takes away from our ability to socialize from person to person making it more difficult to be accepted in social settings. It has become more convenient for us to communicate through texting and our relationships with people and our

ability to communicate have diminished because of it, harming our need of esteem, and our need of love
and acceptance, and if we cant fulfill those needs then we cant fulfill our need for self-actualization.

What are the harms of technology?

Nowadays, we face serious threats such as cyber terrorists, viruses, and online predators, not to mention problems it has created with our personal relationships. Now, don't get me wrong, I am not saying that technology is always bad, but there is a such thing as too much of a good thing, and when you have become addicted to something it is too much. Technology may help for educational purposes and for convenience, but it has also created many problems in society. When was the last time you saw the streets filled with people going on walks, flying kites, and just playing outside. Now we would rather stay indoors and debate about it on the internet.

Although disadvantages may be bought from technological society, but technological society's technology can save us when it comes to weather prediction. Weather satellites are working their asses off to track storms and inform meteorologists so that they could predict their magnitude in advance. The satellites estimate and tell weather experts the storms' strength and how dangerous it is. When a gigantic storm is on its way to consume lives, weather satellites can notify weather experts, defending the people with the shield of modern technology. Hurricanes are extremely destructive, and can cause serious damages. We can not avoid having them, but we can get away from it. what do this job of making people capable of running away from it? The weather satellites are doing that, which are one of the most notable feats that modern technology has achieved. Certainly, in this issue, the positive outweigh the negative.

What technology influences medical treatment as well as brings benefit to our information society?

Cancer is the type of disease that gets its job done. It kills its victims almost certainly, and a diagnosis of cancer is practically a death sentence. This terrifying disease is composed of these vicious cells that grow and divide beyond the normal limits, making cancer incurable. People, even when hospitals
were not equipped with decent medical devices, were cured from some diseases, but they, nine times out of ten, died when cancer got in their way. Although cancer is known as an incurable disease, there are some cases of

people surviving it. The notable thing is that most of these people are cured in present days,

in which technology for medical treatments such as MRI and oxygen inhaler have developed a lot. This hints that technology has taken a big part of making this happy situation possible. If we value convenience, then, technology gives us convenience. Thus, technology is valuable.

Because people are naturally lazy and value efficiency and convenience, technology has become of great practical value. If you use anything that requires the power of electricity in order to work, you are using what modern technology has achieved. When we did not have any proper modern conveniences-internet, computers, automobiles, and iPods- people used to bear the discomforts. They could not travel far and fast since there was no technology to build cars, trains or planes. They often were not capable of storing food well enough for winter so they died of hunger.

In the present day, we get to the other side of the earth in less than 24hours, and can buy any sorts of food in any season. One of the most notable and significant feats that modern technology has achieved is computers. Computers are very useful. People with handicaps can use specially made computers to communicate with people and study. Computers are not just used by humans, but are frequently used by machines to function. Cars, robots and a lot of other high-tech devices have computers installed in them. Without computers, they will be just useless chunk of metals. When we talk about computers, internet takes a huge part of it. Not only does internet allow us the access to tons of information, it also helps us to communicate with our families that are far away. For example, you can e-mail your relatives, and have them answered in an absurdly shot time. Technologies can be very helpful if put together well. Like this, technology has supported our lives and lead us to the new world full of comfort by accomplishing amazing feats.

Just as we value convenience, so we value security, and technology has helped us here, too. The advancements in making weaponries have come a long way. First, our ancestors created weapons such as swords and spears, and other primeval weapons, and as time elapsed, deadly weapons like guns and cannons began to appear on the surface of Earth. As our technology got even better, weapons became much stronger and it came down to what we have now, Atomic weaponries. Of course developing atomic weaponries can have fatal consequences all over the nation, but such cases are rare. Although it can be dangerous, it will enrich our lives if masterfully handled, making it possible to put a dead stop to wars and other threats.

As mentioned earlier, everything has negative effects on us if you look from a critical point of view. If looked from a point of view like that, even believing in God can affect our lives in a negative way. For example, you have to give up your precious time that you could use to study or work to celebrate the special days such as Christmas. Another instance would be attending school and studying since you will be missing the freedom you could have if you did not attend school. Like this, we have to understand that we have to bear some negative factors. Yes, problems come with everything, including technology. However, these problems are of lesser weight than the rewards, and we can even see them as positive because they challenge society to protect our values. For instance, 911 terror produced major damages to America, but now that Americans know that it could happen again, they build buildings

better, and they strengthen the counter terrorist force, resulting in safer lives for Americans. Technologies have done considerable harm in our lives, but they enrich our lives, and are definitely required for better lives of safety, health, and convenience. Life without technology is like a bicycle with only one pedal. It may work, but not well.

If information society can prove that on a scale technology does equal to or more damage as it does good in our lives then the con wins this debate. Then I will indicate some evidences to support my own arguments concern information society can bring positive influence to consumer behavior as below:

.

Positive supportive point: Technology helps different countries farmers to predict whether when weather can provide good growing environment to decide grow enough amount of vegetable, tomato, potato, fruit etc. plant food for human to buy to eat in order to avoid food shortage or food excess waste problem in any time, because fresh food can not be stored long time and if food is stored long time, then perish food will influence our health if the farmers and food business, e.g. supermarkets or food stores still sell perish food when there are many excess food existence in global farming market. Even whether is the suitable weather for cotton growing. So, information society can give more accurate weather information to let farmers to know whether the climate is suitable to grow any foods to avoid food excess growing or shortage problem.

But illnesses related to weight problems are catching up fast. A poor diet and physical inactivity accounted for 400,000 deaths in 2000, some 16.6% of the total. That figure was one-third higher than in 1990." http://www.buzzle.com...

While medical advancements and technology does save lives it is a double edged sword just like with most technological advances.

With the creation of life saving medicine comes the ability to abuse medicine and become addicted to it. For example, Anti-biodics can save someone's life but the more anti-biodics you take the less anti-bodies your body produces because it adapts to the anti-biodics your body is taking in. Then due to your lack of anti-bodies, you are more capable of becoming ill and needing more anti-biodics and the death spiral continues until you completely rely on the drugs to keep you alive.

While cancer is the 3rd leading cause of death in America. "People, even when hospitals were not equipped with decent medical devices, were cured from some diseases, but they, nine times out of ten, died when cancer got in their way." My opponent stresses cancer for some reason but the fact is that technology can only save 9 out of 10 of these victims. Because medical technology is like , it cannot outweigh the harms of technology that I will address later on. Convenience is valuable, but how can you miss something that you've never had? I'm sure people in the seventies weren't depressed because they couldn't have ipods (smart phone), and therefore the quality of life for them was not effected by technology because the technology they were missing out on didn't exist.

At this point I would like to cross-apply my second point "Maslow's Hierarchy of Needs." Or the things we need to live a happy and fulfilling life.

Once again technology is not what makes the quality of our lives better. It is the fulfillment of physiological, safety, acceptance, esteem, and self-actualization needs that makes the quality of our lives better. If anything, technology harms our ability to fulfill these needs. I will start with safety. Nothing is safe anymore, "don't talk to strangers" never used to be a rule that parents gave to their children. Now parents have to be constantly concerned about online predators kidnapping and raping their children. Technology has magnified safety concerns. War used to be men marching with guns and face to face battles, now it consists of threats to blow full nations off the face of the earth, killing innocent civilians everywhere. The more technology that is created the easier it is to destroy a life. So, it seems that information society can bring safe feeling to us.

Next is acceptance, it's difficult to be accepted in a social setting if you never leave the house and learn social skills. Kids used to play outside, now obesity rates are souring, and people have more text and IM conversations than face to face or even over the phone conversations.

Next is esteem, you cant have a strong self esteem if you don't feel accepted, and cant form normal relationships. Lastly self actualization is damaged by technology because we no longer need to do anything. Having the feeling of being born to accomplish something doesn't exist in the minds of people these days. It's all routine, we do everything over the computer and take whatever we can get while putting in the least amount of effort possible. I would attack my opponents fourth point "security is valued" but I already did when I defended the need of safety in my view.

Now to briefly support my own points: An addiction of technological effect in our nowadays information society. An addiction to anything is not good. In a world where obesity is the second biggest killer behind smoking, and when the world could end if our computers stop working, there is too much reliance on technology, and it has created more problems than it is able to fix.

A weather satellite is a type of satellite that is primarily used to monitor the weather and climate of the Earth. Satellites can be either polar orbiting, seeing the same swath of the Earth every 12 hours, or geostationary, hovering over the same spot on Earth by orbiting over the equator while moving at the speed of the Earth's rotation. These meteorological satellites, however, see more than clouds and cloud systems. City lights, fires, effects of pollution, auroras, sand and dust storms, snow cover, ice mapping, boundaries of ocean currents, energy flows, etc., are other types of environmental information collected using weather satellites.

Other environmental satellites can detect changes in the Earth's vegetation, sea state, ocean color, and ice fields. For example, the 2002 oil spill off the northwest coast of Spain was watched carefully by the European ENVISAT, which, though not a weather satellite, flies an instrument (ASAR) which can see changes in the sea surface.

Its effects on weather are monitored daily from satellite images. The Antarctic ozone hole is mapped from weather satellite data. Collectively, weather satellites flown by the U.S., Europe, India, China, Russia, and Japan provide nearly continuous observations for a global weather watch.The field of meteorology entered the space age on April 1, 1960 with the launch of

TIROS 1 (TIROS stands for Television and Infra-Red Observation Satellite). Since that time, numerous satellites with ever increasing capabilities and sophistication have been deployed.

Weather satellites provide valuable real-time cloud photographs. Most importantly, coverage includes the 70 percent of the earth's surface covered by water where few surface observations can be made. Before the deployment of weather satellites, many areas had no advance warning of impending severe storms. Today satellites can spot and accurately track hurricanes and typhoons while they are still far out in the ocean. Modern satellites also carry many instruments used to measure various environmental variables, providing vital information to not only meteorologists, but farmers, geologists, fishermen, foresters and others

How technology impacts weather satellites predict when we are encountering information society stage?

Radiation measurements from the earth's surface and atmosphere give information on the earth-atmosphere energy budget. Measurements from the ocean surface are translated into sea-surface temperatures - information valuable to the fishing industry as well as meteorologists Satellites can monitor snow cover in winter, ice fields in the Arctic and Antarctic, and the height of the ocean's surface. Infrared sensors on satellites can assess conditions of crops, areas of deforestation and regions of drought. Some satellites are equipped with a water vapor sensor that can profile the distribution of water vapor in the atmosphere. Volcanic eruptions and the motion of ash clouds can be detected.

During the winter, satellites monitor the southward progress of freezing air in Florida and Texas, allowing forecasters to warn growers of impending low temperatures. Satellites can receive environmental information from remote data collection platforms on the surface. These include instrumented buoys, river gauges, automatic weather stations, siesmic and tsunami stations, and ships. This information is then relayed to a central receiving station at Wallop's Island, Virginia. So, information society can bring weather prediction and space development benefits to our future.

After reading , how could you say that this topic is "too narrow to be significant"? Satellites greatly add to our knowledge of weather patterns and other environmental factors that affect us all. Regarding to my another issue of medical treatments when we encountering information society stage, are not true all the time. You said, "With the creation of life saving medicine comes the ability to abuse medicine and become addicted to it. For example, Anti-biodics can save someone's life but the more anti-biodics you take the less anti-bodies your body produces because it adapts to the anti-biodics your body is taking in. Then due to your lack of anti-bodies, you are more capable of becoming ill and needing more anti-biodics and the death spiral continues until you completely rely on the drugs to keep you alive." So, it seems that information society can also being high technological development for medical development benefit, instead of space development benefit.

I'm sure people in the seventies weren't depressed because they couldn't have ipods" When I talked about ipods, I was giving it as a general example, covering all the discomforts came from listening to the old-fashioned radio.

I am sure that people did have discomforts and complains about their listening devices. You might say that they could not have complained about such things since they did not even know that such things were going to be invented, but hey, we complain about stuff like oil prices when no brilliant solutions are present. "Once again technology is not what makes the quality of our lives better" Quality of life is the degree of well-being felt by an individual or group of people. Unlike standard of living, it is not a tangible concept, and so cannot be measured directly. It consists of two components: physical and psychological. The physical aspect includes such things as health, diet, and protection against pain and disease.

As it says, the physical aspect includes such things as health, diet, and protection against pain and disease. Once again, for the protection against pain and disease, the medical treatments based on modern technology come back into the play. Modern technology is saving our asses from the pains and diseases compared to the times when we did not have technology as developed as it is now.

1.-Pills that are made with modern technology can help us in getting back appetite and having a balanced diet.

2.-surgeries with better devices based on modern technology keeps us healthy.

3.-technology used in security reasons such as door locks and such can save us from both physical and mental pain. Your close friends or relative might be attacked from invaders and robbers, causing you a mental pain, and your friend a physical/mental pain if we did not have modern technology to keep us safe.

4.-Again, surgeries and pills can cure diseases. Just because there are diseases that technology can not help to cure, it does not mean that technology has not helped us in enriching our lives. It is because our technology is yet to reach its zenith.

I talks about medical technology, but the fact is that much of the things we use medical technology for are caused by technology. For example, they believe that cancer is even caused by technology. Cancer can be caused by Ionizing Radiation, and Chemical Obesity is largely due to our adaptation to technology, we don't even need to leave our house anymore if we don't want to.

"When I talked about ipods, I was giving it as a general example, covering all the discomforts came from listening to the old-fashioned radio." I was giving a general example as well. I was in no way referring to your example. At the time nobody was dealing with discomforts from listening to the old-fashioned radio. Nobody knew that there was any better, and that is why the quality of the life you live can't be impacted by technology you don't yet have. But, when we are facing technological society, we shall easier accept to use smart phone or ipad non-popular computer products to instead traditional desktop or laptop , mobile , because internet or technological media can change consumers product useful behavior change, such as ipad or smart phone can replace laptop, desktop, mobile phone products. It implies that information society can influence consumer behavior to be changed in possible. The question is that whether it can influence any consumer behavior changing degree whether it is more or less.

My opponent closed with a definition of quality of life that states that there are two aspects to quality of life, physical and psychological. It is for this reason that I find Abraham Maslows Hierarchy of Needs a good basis for us to debate upon.

First pills made with modern technology to help us diet are only necessary because of our rising obesity issue that is directly linked to technology. Second, many surgeries that we have are given only because technology exists.

We have become addicted to technology, and can no longer live without it. My opponent never refuted this fact and accepted it as
an inherent danger to our society.

Maslows Hierarchy of Needs.

Maslow gave us five needs for the quality of our lives to be good. Information society can satisfy both physical and mental aspects of our raising quality of life need.

The Inherent Harms of Technology

I gave several good examples, such as cyber terrorism, nuclear warfare, obesity, online predators, and technology adaptation throughout this round as harms of technology, but I have one more specific example of technology gone wrong. I don't know how many people have heard about the Chernobyl disaster, and it would be difficult to summarize it in a debate. Basically in the Soviet Union they buried a bunch of their nuclear weapons equipment and such in a big hole with a concrete shelter, the shelter cracked and there is an underground lake below where they buried it and if the wall of the reactor building or the roof of the shelter were to collapse, then large amounts of radioactive dust and particles would be released directly into the atmosphere, resulting in a large new release of radioactivity into the environment.

In conclusion, I negate this resolution because we have become addicted to technology, it is not a necessity to our fulfillment and happiness in life, and it does more damage than it does good. Technology is not what improves our quality of life or in other words makes it better, and even if it were, the bad that comes with technology is at the least equal if not outweighs the good technology provides.

CHAPTER FIVE

Information society impacts high technological products consumption behaviors

Can information society impact high technological products consumption behavior? If it can, how it impacts our social consumption behavior? What is its degree to impact our consumption behavior in our society? To answer this question, we needs to know why computer is important to influence our social information nowadays. Internet is one digital market tool, it is the most popular technological information tool to influence consumer behavior. I shall explain how and why information society has close relationship to influence consumer behavior as these steps: First, I shall explain what our computer role is nowadays, then I shall explain what the four main factors to influence consumer behavior. Next, I shall apply the Information Processing Models of Consumer Behavior to explain how and why internet (digital market tool) can influence consumer behavior, during the consumer apply this channel to gather any information concerns his purchase choice from internet. Finally, I shall conclude what the effects of the impact of Social Networking on consumer behavior. To evaluate whether we are facing information society, we can attempt to find whether below industries have high technological productivity and raising efficient changes as below:

What is role or computer or internet to different aspect? It is known that the rapid growth of computer usage time. In all areas have been using computers to launch a business.

Role of computer in business

The use of computers among maximum practiced in the field of business. In fact, small businesses also use the computer as there are now

very cheap microcomputers. Business organizations now have a number of facts and a lot of numbers to be processed. So many businesses have started using
the computer, for example to calculate the salary, to identify the goods sold and are still in stock, to issue and send or receive business statements, letters, invoices and more. The use of computers and office equipment to assist other managers, clerks, and the management of office automation mentioned.

One of them is a word processing type of electronic method that enables us to produce and edit letters, reports, documents, and other than work in a few seconds to type manually. Many of the office to produce standard letters, such as payment of the balance, invitations and more. In addition, local business organizations to use computers to create, save, and send envoys to a particular place. The advantages of using computers in this area, clearly it is very important in a business organization.

Role of Computers in Banking and Financial

Processing data involving savings accounts, fixed deposits, loans, investments, profitability analysis, and so on are among the organizations operating budget. The measures used are standard and recurrent. And with that, the financial institution is the first user is aware of the importance of computers to save time. Use of financial institutions including electronic fund transfer activities for example a bank has a terminal in each branch in the country and also in supermarkets, petrol stations, schools, factories, homes, hotels, and so on.

The company will move employees' salary into the account by entering employee identification numbers then pay the money transferred into the
account supermarkets, hotels, or gas station when making a purchase. Money transfer facility is referred to the electronic transfer of money is very
effective use is safe and quick method for financial transactions. With the facility, known as ETC is also individual can issue, transfer, and include cash or checks to the current balance at any time. Clearly the main purpose of the use of computers in financial institutions can assist in arranging the affairs of clients and provide services better and more efficient, reduce fraud in financial transactions also eliminate cash transactions involving the community with the goal to create a cashless society.

Role of Computers in Industrial Areas

Industry is a lot of benefit from the use of computers and the development of a human machine that 'robot'. Industrial production, for example requires a lot of computers to process data collected from employees, customers, sales, product information, production schedules, and so on. Yes said the computer used to control the production process. Especially the production of information processing inventory control to keep the latest information about the remaining inventory of raw materials and finished goods used to determine the value of inventory and stock status. This computer can alert the staff involved if he should order the raw materials and when to deliver the goods completed to the customer. Similarly, to store information about the structure of an item, but the material requirement planning processes also use computers to facilitate the work. Appear in the computer industry is very broad and also affect the development of industry in a country.

Role of Computers in Education

Now in this era of science and technology become more advanced, the computer may take over the role of books in the store and disseminate knowledge to the public. In other words, the computer will change the way we learn and the way we store knowledge. Hal-related matters such as student registration, class scheduling, processing of examination results, students 'and teachers' personal storage can be implemented by a computer with a fast and effective in helping the administration. Now exams results were processed by computer. The IPT also the duties of office automation, processing, scientific research results and also use the computer.

In fact, cataloging books in libraries also apply to computer use. Last but not least is used for teaching and learning process is not only at institutions of higher learning in the schools, both for teaching and studying computer-assisted education on computer is very emphasized that in the field of education for helping in the administrative process, research is what is important is the ease and help students and teachers in the teaching and learning.

Role of Computers in the Medical

Hospitals and clinics use computers to store patient records, scheduling doctors, nurses and other personnel, inventory and purchase of medicines, medical research and medical diagnosis. Applications of computer-based equipment or use of information technology has help doctors to diagnose diseases. It is clear that the use of computers in the medical field to provide solutions to complex problems. Among the new computer technology that provides assistance to those who are disabled. Microprocessor-based voice systems assist people with disabilities speaking with a terminal that directs the computer to perform a verbal task.

Similarly, the development of computers has helped the blind to see, the deaf to communicate, whether with the help of speech synthesizer or using the keyboard. This can be help them become more active and can do what they could not do before. Besides works of traditional data processing, such as issuing bills of patients,
medical statistics and scheduling of staff and others have also streamlined and processed by computer. Hospital Information System that is used can be stored in a centralized patient database.

In fact, the use of information technology the computer is programmed to culture and analyze bacteria, viruses, and other infections agents to automatically detect and identify a disease thus enabling the hospitals and laboratories to begin treatment. For example, Computer Help Demography machine (Computer Aided Demography, CAT) used for the purpose. Similarly, computers are used for a patient oversee psychological variables such as blood pressure, body temperature, ECG (Electro-Cardiograph) and sounded a warning if something unusual happens. For this purpose the computer to read different variables and make comparison with standard values. If there is something extraordinary happens the computer will draw the attention of doctors and nurses to issue a warning. Clearly, it was found that the computer has a wide range of accommodation in the medical field.

Role of Computers in Legal

Computers have been used in the legislative process in recent years. The use of the most important is the preparation of documents using a word processor. The use of computer accounting legislation also includes processing to produce weekly and monthly reports, keep records of payments consulting, diary for the latest attorney information consumers about the various court procedures and also to keep records of users. As this area is very complicated, it is the need to retrieve the required information either on journal of law, an important case, scale, and statistics or important decisions for the purpose of making the decision to retain legal data bank. Thus the use of one computer will help lawyers and trainee lawyers and law students find relevant data without wasting time and get better service.

Role of Computers in Government

Government sector is one of the largest users of computer usage practices in implementing administrative matters. All the necessary data can be obtained in a short time such as information about people, services, economic planning, and land development projects and for planning and decision making. Through long-term weather forecasting computer can now be done. With tie loss of life can be because of better information and faster. "The success of Neil Am strong on July 23, 1969 landing on the moon is also made possible with the help of computers used to design spacecraft, space for clothes astronauts, and flight schedules". This shows the very important use of computers in the field of space transportation. Service tax and income tax collection was simplified by

using the computer. Keeping records of taxpayers who do it manually, and bring many problems have been addressed with the use of computer and services can make

the task more efficiently and quickly.

Similarly, in the military, use of computer store inventory held until the war simulation on the screen. Computers are also used to follow the movement of the enemy in the border areas. Traffic flow can be managed effectively by detecting the direction of traffic using the many tools of detection. In this way, if there are more vehicles from one direction, the computer will let the green light goes on for a suitable period of time. "In the field of transport, Cosmos- 11 introduced by Mass by providing facilities for passengers to know the status including those booking hotel reservations, from anywhere in the world". Similarly, business owners and vehicle registration can be performed with the use of computers. Many of the all administrative affairs are managed by using the computer. This not only saves time but can do all things more practical.

Role of Computers in entertainment

Now the computer can be programmed to play music. Places of entertainment with music controlled by computer are cheaper and can be used at any time.

Computers are also used to arrange the order of dance and music. Each game requires movement. Movement can best be obtained by detailed analysis of a physical system. Computers also can be programmed to depict images of high quality. Drawing using the computer speeds up the process of creating. The work of art can be done and made a

review in a short time compared with traditional Kedah. Cartoon films produced by computers have grown so widely.

Role of Computers at daily life

Microcomputer use also home to control the safety and control of air conditioning and lighting. The use of computers in the home allows housewife get the latest information about fashion and can make orders to use supermarket with and video. In addition to budget planning and inventory at home. This is all to do with a microcomputer that is connected to the national data bank. Children can use computers to learn school subjects or educational games. But it is clear that computers have become machines of information in our society.

The rapid development of science and technology has changed the pattern of life now. Everything, processing, gathering information, or any aspects of the various areas that were previously done manually, which gives a lot of risk has to be made more effective, faster, and more practical with the application or use of information technology or computer. Covering the use in various fields including business, financial institutions, industry, education, administration and other fields have the desire to realize develop each country. The fact is, computers have become the heart and backbone of society today. Whatever the field, computing has a lot of people taken over the task. It will not only help in the calculations, store information, detect a decision also to increase efficiency and productivity. But they said it is now clear that the use of computers has been widely practiced and used.

In line with globalization and the borderless world, the computer is a machine in the information society is also the main artery of all machinery administration in any field. I believe it offers an escape route – but only if these micro-level projects are nurtured, promoted and protected by a fundamental change in what governments do. And this must be driven by a change in our thinking – about technology, ownership and work. So that, when we create the elements of the new system, we can say to ourselves, and to others: "This is no longer simply my survival mechanism, my bolt hole from the neoliberal world; this is a new way of living in the process of formation."

Economy Report indicated that the 2008 crash wiped 13% off global production and 20% off global trade. Global growth became negative – on a scale where anything below +3% is counted as a recession. It produced, in the west, a depression phase longer than in 1929-33, and even now, amid a pallid recovery, has left mainstream economists terrified about the prospect of long-term stagnation. The aftershocks in Europe are tearing the continent

apart. The solutions have been austerity plus monetary excess. But they are not working. In the worst-hit countries, the pension system has been destroyed, the retirement age is being hiked to 70, and education is being privatized so
that graduates now face a lifetime of high debt. Services are being dismantled and infrastructure projects put on hold.

Even now many people fail to grasp the true meaning of the word "austerity". Austerity is not eight years of spending cuts, as in the UK, or even the social catastrophe inflicted on Greece. It means driving the wages, social wages and living standards in the west down for decades until they meet those of the middle class in China and India on the way up. Meanwhile in the absence of any alternative model, the conditions for another crisis are being
assembled. Real wages have fallen or remained stagnant in Japan, the southern Eurozone, the US and UK. The shadow banking system has been reassembled,
and is now bigger than it was in 2008. New rules demanding banks hold more reserves have been watered down or delayed.

So, the first economic model in 200 years the upswing of which was premised on the suppression of wages and smashing the social power and resilience of the working class. If we review the take-off periods studied by long-cycle theorists – the 1850s in Europe, the 1900s and 1950s across the globe – it was the strength of organized labor that forced entrepreneurs and corporations to stop trying to revive outdated business models through wage cuts, and to innovate their way to a new form of capitalism.

The result is that, in each upswing, we find a synthesis of automation, higher wages and higher-value consumption. Today there is no pressure from the workforce,
and the technology at the center of this innovation wave does not demand the creation of higher-consumer spending, or the resign employment of the old workforce in new jobs. Information is a machine for predicting or measuring the price of things (products) lower and slashing the work time needed to support life on the planet.

As a result, faced with the possibility of creating gene-sequencing labs, they instead start coffee shops, nail bars and contract cleaning firms: the banking system, the planning system and late neoliberal culture reward above all the creator of low-value, long-hours jobs. Innovation is happening but it has not, so far, triggered the fifth long upswing for capitalism that long-cycle theory would expect. The reasons lie in the specific nature of information technology.

We're surrounded not just by intelligent machines but by a new layer of reality centered on information. Consider an airliner: a computer flies it; it has been designed, stress-tested and "virtually manufactured" millions of times; it is firing back real-time information to its manufacturers. On board are people squinting at screens connected, in some lucky countries, to the internet. Seen from the ground it is the same white metal bird as in the James Bond era. But it is now both an intelligent machine and a node on a network. It has an information content and is adding "information value" as well as physical value to the world. On a packed business flight, when everyone's peering at Excel or Powerpoint, the passenger cabin is best understood as an information factory.

How any why information society can impact human consumption behaviors ? To answer this question, we need to know what the main factors can influence consumer behavior.

Consumer Behavior means that the consumer is someone who pays a sum to consume the goods and services sold by an organization. The consumer plays a very important role in the demand and supply chain of every economic system of every nation. The producers of the goods and services would lack the motive of producing as there would be no demand for their products. A number of terms in current use emphasize related but different aspects of the emerging global economic order. The Information Society intends to be the most encompassing in that an economy is a subset of a society. The Information Age is somewhat limiting, in that it refers to a 30-year period between the widespread use of computers and the knowledge economy, rather than an emerging economic order. The knowledge era is about the nature of the content, not the socioeconomic processes by which it will be traded. The computer revolution, and knowledge revolution refer to specific revolutionary transitions, rather than the end state towards which we are evolving. The Information Revolution relates with the well known terms agricultural revolution and industrial revolution.

Who is a consumer?

A consumer need not just be an individual; a consumer can also be an organization. A consumer can be someone who will buy either goods or services or you can also specify the goods and services as economic services or products, or good or commodities. A consumer is the end user or a target to whom the goods and services are sold. In simple words a consumer can be described as:

1.A person or an organization that is specifically targeted to sell a products or a service of a company.

OR

2.Someone again, mind you this someone can either be an individual or an organization that pays a price to use the goods and services of an organization.

OR

3.A person or an organization who is the final user of the goods and the services produced by a company.

OR

You can consider all three definitions to define a consumer.

The consumer is the decision maker here in the economic system. He can take the following decisions

1.The decision of buying or not a product in a store or at a shop.

2.The consumer will decide if he would want to be influenced by the marketing strategies and the advertisements of the organization for a product or a service.

3.Many consumers are influenced by marketing and advertisements.

4.The consumer decides what they want to buy and when they want to buy it.

5.The consumer chooses between competitors and their products.

Decision making is the power given to the consumer.

Everyone has been a consumer and participated in the consumer market. The consumer market is where the consumer has the right and the power to make a decision of spending their money. Even buying a packet of chips from a store is being a part of the consumer market as you participate in the buying a packet of chips buy paying a sum for the purchase. Here you are also taking a decision. This is a decision of buying goods and spending your money. You are deciding where to spend your money and on what should you spend your money. You are deciding amongst competitors.

The more active the consumers of the nation the more active will be the nation's consumer market.

Consumer behavior is a physiological process it is all related to the emotions of the consumer. In this process the consumer starts with recognizing the need of the product, and then finds a way or a medium of solving these needs, makes purchase decisions like planning whether he should buy or not buy a certain product, and then he confirms the information, jots down a plan and then implements the plan of making the purchase.

Consumer behavior is physiological it is human behavior it can change with the slightest change in the market, the atmosphere and the trend. Studying consumer behavior is a challenge take look at a few challenges that is how can you study consumer behavior

How to ensure whether information society can influence consumer behavior?

1.The online consumer psychology is different when they shop and make decisions of spending their money from store shopping.

2.How can the online store motivate the consumer buying behavior, helping him make a decision in selecting between products from ecommerce channel?

3.Why should the company feel need to improve their online sale strategy based on their focused consumer behavior?

4.How does a single online consumer decision effects a group of online consumers that is a group of people, this can include their friends, their family, etc.

5.How a single or a group of online consumer behavior does affects the society and the atmosphere and the economy of the nation.

What are the types of consumer behavior?

(1) Programmed or routine behavior

Buying of regular and daily goods that involve very less money and also minimum research work fits under this type of goods buying behavior.
For example buying goods from the grocery store that are goods used on daily basis like milk, eggs, bread, etc.

(2) Buying products occasionally or limited decision making

When a consumer tries to gain information about unfamiliar brands of familiar products of not very high value goods this is when a consumer makes a decision however occasionally. The time required to gather such information is quite moderate for example buying of goods like clothes and cosmetics.

(3) Complex and involvement or extensive decision making

Buying of products such as computers, laptops, property, cars, education, etc which requires a huge amount of research and economic involvement comes under this category or type. This decision take time as it needs too much of research work as the consumer will study almost
all the options available in his economic range, the research is prolonged as the customer would want to buy the best option available for the price he is paying.

(4) The last type is the impulse buying or the conscious planning type

The job of the organizations here is to educate the consumers about their goods and services and motivate them to buy their goods and services. Predicting single or consumer of a group is not just difficult because you never know what factors might influence them and when.

Reason being the consumers today have a huge variety of choice and a number of factors influence the behavior of the online shopping method as below:

The information economy and the knowledge economy emphasize the content or intellectual property that is being traded through an information market or knowledge market, respectively. Electronic commerce and electronic business emphasize the nature of transactions and running a business, respectively, using the Internet and World-Wide Web. The digital economy focuses on trading bits in cyberspace rather than atoms in physical space. The network economy stresses that businesses will work collectively in webs or as part of business ecosystems rather than as stand-alone units. Social networking refers to the process of collaboration on massive, global scales. The internet economy focuses on the nature of markets that are enabled by the Internet.

Knowledge services and knowledge value put content into an economic context. Knowledge services integrates Knowledge management, within a Knowledge organization, that trades in a Knowledge market. In order for individuals to receive more knowledge, surveillance is used. This relates to the use of Drones as a tool in order to gather knowledge on other individuals. Although seemingly synonymous, each term conveys more than nuances or slightly different views of the same thing. Each term represents one attribute of the likely nature of economic activity in the emerging post-industrial society.

Alternatively, the new economic order will incorporate all of the above plus other attributes that have not yet fully emerged. In connection with the development of the information society, appeared information pollution, evolving information ecology - associated with information hygiene. Today, It is important to selectively select the information. Due to information revolution, the amount of information is puzzling. Among these, we need to develop techniques that refine information. This is called data mining. It is an engineering term, but it is used in sociology. In other words, if the amount of information was competitive in the past, the quality of information is important today.

What are important factors that influence consumer behavior in our information society nowadays ?

You for sure might be wondering as to what is it that influences these consumers, how do we analyzes when is their purchase pattern going to change. Of course only the influencing factors will confirm what will change the consumers buying pattern.

We have four main factors that affect consumer behavior they are;

1.Consumer Behavior – Cultural factors

Culture plays a very vital role in the determining consumer behavior it is sub divided in. Culture is a very complex belief of human behavior it includes the human society, the roles that the society plays, the behavior of the society, its values customs and traditions. Culture needs to be examined as it is a very important factor that influences consumer behavior.

Sub-Culture

Sub-culture is the group of people who share the same values, customs and traditions. You can define them as the nation, the religion, racial groups and also groups of people sharing the same geographic location.

Social Class

Society possesses social class; in fact every society possesses one. It is important to know what social class is being targeted as normally the
buying behavior of a social class is quite similar. Remember not just the income but even other factors describe social class of a group of consumers.

2.Consumer Behavior – Social Factors

Social factors are also subdivided into the following

Reference groups

Under social factors reference groups have a great potential of influencing consumer behavior. Of course its impact varies across products and brands.

This group often includes an opinion leader.

Family

The behavior of a consumer is not only influenced by their motivations and personalities but also their families and family members who can two or

more people living together either because of blood relationship or marriage.

Role and status

People who belong to different organizations, groups or club members, families play roles and have a status to maintain. These roles and status that they have to maintain also influences consumer behavior as they decide to spend accordingly.

3.Consumer Behavior – Personal factors

A number of personal factors also influence the consumer behavior. In fact this is one major factor that influences consumer behavior.
The sub factors under personal factor are listed below.

Age and life cycle stage

Age of a consumer and his life cycle are two most important sub factors under personal factors. With the age and the life cycle the consumers purchase options and the motive of purchase changes, with his decisions of buying products change. Hence this stage does affect consumer behavior.

Occupation

Occupation of a consumer is affects the goods and services a consumer buys. The occupations group has above average interest in buying different products and services offered by organizations. In fact organizations produce separate products for different occupational groups.

Financial or economic situations

Everything can be bought and sold with the help of money. If the economic situation of a consumer is not good or stable it will affect his purchase power, in fact if the consumers or the economy of a nation is suffering a loss it defiantly affects the consumers purchase or spending decisions.

Life style

People originating from different cultures, sub cultures, occupations and even social class have different styles of living. Life style can confirm the interest, opinions and activities of people. Different life styles affect the purchase pattern of consumers.

Self concept and personality

Every individual is different and have different and distinct personalities. Their distinct personalities and distinct physiology effects their buying decisions.

Hence purchase of products and services defers from person to person.

4.Consumer Behavior – Psychological factors

Psychological factors affect consumer behavior very strongly, such as this topic discuss whether information society how influence consumer behavior, e.g. internet , this high technological tool can be used to gather any product information to satisfy consumers information gathering need by consumers learning, motivation and attitude factors influence. When they prefer to choose internet information more than newspapers, TV , radio, magazine advertisement information to seek any product information.

Motivation

Motivation is activating the internal needs and requirements of the consumer. It can also be described as goals and needs of the consumers. Motivation arouses and directs the consumers towards certain goals. These needs can be psychological needs, needs of security, social needs,

esteem needs and also self actualizing needs, e.g. online shopping can let the consumer feel convenience, easier gathering product photo and price and gradient information to make comparison.

Perception

Perception is sensing the world and the situations around and then taking a decision accordingly. Every individual look as the world and the situations differently. The judging ability and capacity of every individual is different and hence the look at the world differently. This is what separates the decision taking abilities.

Learning and experience

Learning is the research of products and services before the consumer takes the decision of buying a product. Learning and self educating these days is done online and also in groups. Experience is taking a lesson from the past experiences of a product and service. Learning and experience both again play an important role in influencing the consumer's behavior as it influences their purchase decision.

Attitude and beliefs

Attitude is a consumer's favorable and unfavorable emotional condition or emotional feeling, also its tendency of reaction to certain actions and behaviors. Beliefs of people that are the belief that people assume the products to be as make the specifications of the products. Hence attitude and beliefs are also important and need to be taken into consideration while studying human behavior.

How Technology And Its Impact On Consumer Behavior ?

Often a company leadership faces unending challenges especially when it comes to the rapid technological changes. Since the emergence of information technology, company communication with its customers took a turn to an unknown destination. Just think back ten years ago or even 5 years, how were businesses reaching their customers? How were customers reaching them? Compare that to how communication is passing between the two parties now and who is driving it.

Technology has placed the power in the customers' hands literally with the internet enabled smart phone and tablets. Note, that these devices are always being improved such that the newest version offers more to the consumers, making the previous one obsolete in as little as six months' time.

How and why has technology changed the way consumers behave? Here are a few things that you need to keep in mind as you reinvent your strategies to keep up with the consumers.

(1) Customers are connected

Almost everybody is living two lives, a vibrant online life and a somewhat boring offline one. We are all connected in one platform or another through our network of friends. We also own more than one device that keeps us updated. This means that we thrive on being active and informed online, and Exact Target Marketing content verified this from a study they did, whereby 91% of consumers indicated that access to content across all devices was important.Information technology advancements fuel the connectivity that brings together the world as one big community, from the smart phones to super-fast data. This trend is not about to change because now kids as young as 5 years know how to operate a smart phone, LinkedIn even lowered its age limit to 13years to capitalize on the technology adoption rate.

Companies need to meet the consumers where they are and satisfy their sophisticated needs. If your target market spends more time on Instagram or Twitter, be present and respond to them on the same platform. Are you doing enough to leverage technology and handle the informed consumer?

(2) Consumer expectations have changed

In the past, as a company you set the times that you were open for business, and customers had to put up with it or stay without that particular product. Technology has totally changed that, with the introduction of e-commerce and mobile phones, customers can access products at anytime. They have raised expectations on what is acceptable customer service and what is not. As a business, you have to keep up with the changed consumer behavior or be out of business, for example, if a customer wants to purchase something online at night and has a query, they expect to get instant answers. If they do not they choose another supplier from the myriad available online who can meet their immediate need. Consumers now understand the power they have and will use it when not satisfied with a service. A simple expression of their dissatisfaction on your social media that is not responded to immediately will ignite uproar from other customers who were OK with your products and service.

(3) New communication channels

In the past, a company provided customer service through emails –that did not get prompt responses – and phone calls. These two communication tools had their own challenges and favored the company more; it was at their discretion what information to give out.This age however, is very refreshed. Social media platforms and live chat place you right in front of your customer; you cannot sacrifice your customer to maintain your brand position. Actually, when you do not respond to a query, you damage your brand reputation because that information is accessible to millions of people. The upside of these new tools is that you have a wider data collection pool; you can fast track your research and development by utilizing the big data.

I shall indicate how one customer decides purchase decision when he applies internet technological tool to gather information in order to make his final rational purchase decision as below:

What is Information Processing Models of Consumer Behavior ?

Nowadays information society, this model concerns every online consumer how to apply internet to gather any product information to do compare in order to decide whether he ought buy which brand of product as well as he ought buy the brand of product from internet channel or store channel , which one is more suitable. Effectively, the internet may influence the any consumer's final purchase decision changes. So that better decisions can be made by marketers within the context of marketing systems, decision making by firms and by consumers must be understood. Descriptive models of consumer behavior, one aspect of this

problem, are the focus in this paper. These are information processing models of individual consumers' grocery product shopping decisions. Information processing models have been successfully applied to other areas of decision making in economics, when the consumer applies internet to gather any products information.

The internet product information seeker will do decision either Accept or Reject when he spends long time to seek any products information from internet channel. Associate risk (bad or good internet information gathering experience) with these food, when the consumer applies internet to gather any information concerns below food or product. The online consumer will ask any one of these questions in his whole internet food or product gathering process as below:

Is this fresh meat, eggs or produce?
Is price justified level?
Is color okay?
Is the price of extra large over 5 cents more than the price of large?
Is this large size?
Is this extra large size?
Was this product bought last time for this product type?
Was last online shopping experience is better or worse to compare this time?
Is risk associated with this product (bad online shopping experience)?
Is this product class high risk?
Is it the cheapest size?
Is this the cheapest?
Had a good experience with any brands in this class?
Did they state a preference this week from their websites ?
Are several "okay" brands cheapest (that they have in stock)?
Have a coupon for this one when purchase online ?

That online choice point processes. Finally, it can fall into three basic categories:

(1) choice object attributes: for example, color, price, weight;
(2) external environmental attributes: in order to limit the scope of the modeling process, such complex matters as
husband or child preference, use experience with a product, or word of mouth are taken as cues processed by the housewife, but are not explained by a detailed model
of their own; internal cues or cognitive variables; the major cue measured here is the degree of risk felt toward a product class .

Given this viewpoint, if a model of an individual's processes is desired, how one infers the structure of these processes is an important question. All above these issues will be every online consumer who concerns whether the seller's website can provide the accurate product information to persuade him/her to make final online shopping choice.

How can the impact of Social Networking on consumer behavior ?

Social media has been used heavily for business purposes while communicating with customers and promoting new products or services. Because there is a direct connection between communications and promotion, social media was easily integrated in the marketing field. Similarly, within marketing, the market research industry has been greatly affected by developments in social media and social communication. The massive growth of the usage of social media affects consumer behavior since there are consumption related interactions in these platforms. Social media and the ability of consumers to consult each other have transformed the traditional brand – consumer relationship, putting the consumer in a clear powerful position. Social media have changed marketing by shifting the scalability of influence and the ways in which consumers share, evaluate and choose information. With the rise of social media such as blogs, online forums and social networks the voice of the consumer becomes stronger and companies realize that marketing to today's technology driven consumers mean engaging in two-way communication. The current research will outline the major changes in consumer behavior and provide recommendations for retailers on how to integrate social media more effectively and improve engagement with their audience.

Based on these reasons, it is easier to understand the massive growth of social media in such short time. Individuals and organizations have embraced the internet and its social elements because of the basic need for communication and interaction that Aristotle mentions. Social media has also been used heavily for business purposes while communicating with customers and promoting new

products or services. Because there is a direct connection between communications and promotion, social media was easily integrated in the marketing field.

Similarly, within marketing, the market research industry has been greatly affected by developments in social media and social communication (Patino, 2012). The first social media site was sixdegrees.com and was established in 1997. Since then, a large number of social media platforms has been launched for personal or business purposes such as

LiveJournal, Ryze.com, Tribe.net, LinkedIn, Friendster, MySpace, Facebook etc. In July 2012, the number of active Facebook users has reached 955 million (Facebook, 2012). The members of the social media channels can be considered as a part of promotion mix and they can provide useful analytics and feedback to firms. Moreover, around 1.5 million businesses average set up on Facebook brand communities such as fan pages for marketing purposes

(Website-Monitoring, 2010).

The study of consumer behavior is relatively new. Before 1960, consumption was an area which belonged to the economic discipline. Since then, consumer research has been rapidly developed. Traditional marketing involved a one-way communication effort. Through public relations and advertising campaigns, companies put forward value propositions to attract and

retain customers and drive sales. The massive growth of the usage of social media affects consumer behavior since there are consumption related interactions in these platforms. Social media and the ability of consumers to consult each other have transformed the

traditional brand – consumer relationship, putting the consumer in a clear powerful position (Christodoulides and Jevons, 2011). In past years, the brand managers had to create inspiring and clear messages, place them in media and hope that consumers would respond and express their preference for the brand and ideally purchase. Social media have changed marketing by shifting the scalability of influence and the ways in which consumers share, evaluate and choose information (Smithee, 2011). With the rise of social media such as blogs, online forums and social networks the voice of the consumer becomes stronger and companies realize that marketing to today's technology driven consumers mean engaging in two-way communication.

Consumer engagement focuses on consumers' needs in order to engage with them. Both concepts are customer-centric approaches that give primacy to the consumer. Sellers can only meet the needs of the buyers, determine what added value is required and how to do it, if they engage with consumers. A one-time purchase or even repeat purchases of the same product does not equal engagement with the customer. It could be evidence that the customer is satisfied with the product or service but even satisfaction and retention does not necessarily signify customer engagement (Sashi, 2012).

Engaged customers are likely to recommend products through blogs, social networking sites or word-of-mouth in a way that they become advocates of the brand. They help sellers understand their needs and contribute actively in the product development process. Through
social media, organizations can establish an advanced communication with existing and potential clients before, during and after the transaction period with information, promotions and new product announcements. The following print screen (Picture 1) is taken from the Facebook page of JeepR Corp. where photos are posted regularly and followers like, comment, share and request further information about the cars of the manufacturer.

Relationships are defined around concepts such as trust, commitment, integrity and value creation. Organizations need to understand the needs and requests of their customers, respond to them and develop relationships with engagement through social media. Sashi defines this as a focus on 'satisfying customers by providing superior value than competitors to build trust and commitment in long term relationships' (Sashi, 2012, p. 260). With the use of social media, marketing strategies can become more customized and targeted as well as cheaper, faster and more international in reach. Social networking represents the evolution of marketing from the marketing concept era to market orientation to relationship marketing.
The interactive nature of social media enables the establishment of conversations between individuals and companies in communities of customers and sellers and involves the first ones to generate content and

value creation. This has resulted companies to try to better serve customers and satisfy faster their needs.

The Social Media Report 2012, which is published by Nielsen and nmIncite (2012), demonstrates the impact of social media to marketers while trying to build their brands and connect with their audience more effectively. Consumers use Social Media to express their
loyalty to favorite brands and products, and many seek to reap benefits from brands for helping promote their products.

How and why can internet advertisement impact consumer behavior ?

It can be said that advertising is a subset "promotions" in the marketing mix decisions and promotions put simply involves the mass communication of the product offering to the target market (Jobber and Ellis-Chadwick, 2013). Other than the obvious reason of persuading customers to make purchases, it is imperative to promote the product offering in order to create an image of the product which becomes one of its differentiating factors (Doyle and Stern, 2006). Furthermore the promotion of a product offering is important to reinforce the information the customers already have about the product (Doyle and Stern, 2006). As mentioned earlier, advertising is one of the components of promoting a product offering and thus it is defined as "the paid presentation and promotion of products or services through mass media such as television, radio, newspapers and the internet"(Doyle and Stern, 2006).

Traditionally, advertising is carried out on the television, radio and in newspapers however disruptive technology like the internet and the phenomena it has made possible has changed advertising and the effect it can have on consumers particularly where it concerns their purchasing decisions (Jobber and Ellis-Chadwick, 2013). Illustrating this point, Google and Facebook have created new environments which are part of the networks to which the planet belongs and which operate at break-neck speed (Jobber and Ellis-Chadwick, 2013). Furthermore, the internet and social networks have also changed the way individuals communicate such that advertisements do not inherently have to be paid – a good review from one consumer to a group of others can be all the advertisement that a company would need (Jobber and Ellis-Chadwick, 2013). In addition to this, advertisements can now be interactive in such a way that the information on the product passed on to the consumer is more targeted and customised (Jobber and Ellis-Chadwick, 2013). Thus this paper will be exploring the impact of online advertisements on consumer purchasing behavior first by outlining the theories of how advertising works, then examining the effects online advertisements on consumer purchasing behavior .

Ehrenberg (cited by Jobber and Ellis-Chadwick, 2013) explaining that advertising can work exactly the way the ATR model theorises as there is no need for strong emotions like desire and conviction before a first purchase is made. It could simply be a purchase for trial followed by reinforcements.

How Online Advertisements and Its Impact on Consumer Purchasing Behavior Suceed?

The beginning on online advertising was in 1994 when Hot Wire sold the first ad banner on their company's website (Bakshi and Gupta, 2013). By year 2000 online advertising spending in the United States had reached $8.2 billion dollars with these numbers increasing to $12.7 billion as more people are connected to the internet and spend more time online (Bakshi and Gupta, 2013). This is a clear sign that online advertising has developed quickly in the last decade. Some of examples of online advertisements includes floating ads, expanding ads, wallpaper ads, trick banners, pop-ups and pop-unders (Bakshi and Gupta, 2013). Now these are the ones instigated by marketers or producers themselves. This paper however puts forward that if advertising (online advertising being no different) is a method of mass-communicating product benefits then online word of mouth or reviews may be considered as an additional method of online advertising albeit the marketers or producers would have very little control as to how such reviews are presented.

Online Reviews

Research has shown that consumer opinion and recommendations actually count towards purchase decision because product review allows consumers to get a feel for the product without making a trial purchase (Murphy, 2015). Recommendation sources according to Andreasen (1968) have a typology as follows: impersonal advocate (mass media), impersonal independent (consumer reports), impersonal advocates (sales clerk) and personal independents (friends) (Senecal and Nantel, 2004). Sencal and Nantel (2004) also report that consumers indicated that for their next purchase of durable goods they would be using first their personal independents as sources of recommendation.

This plays directly to customers' need for information. Whilst customers could research products through search engines such as Google and Bing. It is never quite like having a first hand account from an unbiased user of the product. Statistics have shown that 80% of online shoppers would change their minds based on online reviews (Murphy, 2015). Supporting this is the fact that in a study carried out in India of the influencers of online purchase decisions, 93% of the respondents indicated that they considered online word of mouth much more reliable than all the other sources of information including the typical online ads (Bakshi and Gupta, 2013).

Thus it would logically follow that having bad reviews would correlate with poor sales whereas good reviews would mean good sales (Murphy, 2015). A case in point is the sale for a t-shirt on Amazon which shot up a staggering 2300% in 2009 after a joke review for the T shirt went viral on the internet (Murphy, 2015). Till date the t-shirt which features three wolves howling at a full moon has garnered over 2000 reviews (Murphy, 2015). Another example is a study which showed that the biggest influencer for holiday shopping recommendations was from friends and family on social media with 63% swayed by Amazon reviews and 24% were from blogger endorsements (Morrison, 2014).

Social Media/Social Networks

Directly related to online reviews where it concerns online advertising are social networks which could be considered as the platform through which online reviews are exchanged albeit they should be considered separate elements and influencers (Morrison, 2014). Social network platforms such as Facebook which grew by 22% between October 2011 and November 2011 and Youtube which grew 67% percent between the same time frame are the new age medium of online advertising reaching millions of people at a go (Darban and Li, 2012). A study carried out between 2013 and 2014 found that 64% of respondents were convinced of what holiday gift to purchase by a social medium. Social media appears to be so effective that there is at least one social medium guiding consumers through their path to purchase. For example, 58% of respondents to the aforementioned study used Pinterest to find ideas and inspiration, 60% use Facebook to seek promotion whilst 48% share the the purchases they have made on Facebook inspiring others to also make purchases (Morrison, 2014). To this end, 11 out of 12 respondents confirmed that they have made purchases as a result of interacting with the producers on social media or interacting with their peers on social media and getting a sort of first hand advertisement of the product online (Darban and Li, 2012). In addition consumers have also indicated that they are able to communicate directly with producers via social media thus speeding up the purchase process as they also indicated that the length of time it sometimes takes to get the information they need from producers can put them off buying the product in the first instance (Darban and Li, 2012).

General Online Advertisements

In a study carried out on the effects of online advertisements on consumer buying behavior of branded garments in Pakistan(Afzal and Rabbani Khan, 2015), it was interestingly discovered that there is no direct effect of online advertisements on the buying decisions of branded garments whereas it was found that there is a significant indirect effect of online advertisements on consumer buying decisions because of advertising characteristics and consumer attitudes (Afzal and Rabbani Khan, 2015). Conversely, in another study carried out it was found that contrary to the discovery of the study in Pakistan there was a direct link between online banner advertisements and the making of purchases or purchase decisions (Li and Leckenby, 2004) . Interesting another study showed that revenue garnered as a result of online banner ads (which attracted the most revenue) were on a high from 1998 when 56% of revenue made by the respondent company were from online banner ads. However, by the year 2001 these numbers had began falling until 2003 when it was only at 21% (Li and Leckenby, 2004). These studies did not give the reason as to the decline banner ads generated revenue. However the study in Pakistan had reported that consumers seemed to place more stock on word of mouth such as online reviews and a large percentage of the revenue generated by the participating companies were from loyal customers and referrals (Afzal and Rabbani Khan, 2015). These go back to reiterate the points of discussion in the previous section of this paper as to the effectiveness of social media platforms and online reviews as a method of marketing. Thus it would appear that other methods or forms of online advertisement do not perform as well as social media platforms and online word of mouth it terms of being revenue generators.

The logical question to ask then is why this is so? The answer is not far-fetched and probably lies in the results of a study carried out on consumer perception of online advertisements (Priyanka, 2012). The options provided were entertaining, informative, irritation, credibility, interactivity and purchase. The respondents to these study were further adjusted for age in order to get a clear picture as to the age range of consumers and their perspective (Priyanka, 2012). Of the 100 respondents to the study, irrespective of age, 22 found online advertisements informative, 18 found them irritating whilst 18 respondents have made purchases because of online advertisements (Priyanka, 2012). Of those the respondents who made purchases 6 were between the ages of 41-50 whilst 5 respondents were of the older than 50 age group (Priyanka, 2012). In addition a very small percentage of this age group found online adverts credible which could mean that perhaps if they felt online adverts as more credible they could be looking to making more purchases (Priyanka, 2012). Surprising this age group also found online adverts less irritating but also less informative (Priyanka, 2012). This could logically be reasoned to be as a result of the fact that most purchasers of this age actually want more information before they make purchases and are willing to suffer through online advertisements perhaps because they are not skilled in surfing social media platforms to gain more information of the product (the study also showed that only a very small percentage of the above 50 age group do not surf the internet or engage in online window shopping) (Priyanka, 2012).

Thus it would appear that forms of advertisement other than social media and online word of mouth walk a tight rope of being irritating and putting the consumer off thereby having a negative impact on consumer purchasing decisions.

Other Forms of Advertisements and its Impact on Consumer Purchase Behavior

In a study of 175 respondents carried out by Iqbal et al (2013) to determine the relationship between brand perception, advertising and consumer purchase behavior. Their findings, analysis and results showed that advertisements had a positive effect on brand perception and consumer purchase behavior, particularly in teenage consumers (Iqbal et al, 2013). Similarly Mel et al (cited by Malik et al 2014) argues that over time, advertisement plays a major role in influencing the consumer such that they become less price sensitive. In the same vein, Ackerbergm (cited by Malik et al, 2014) also argues that advertising is a great source of product learning for consumers. However image advertising and prestige advertising appears to have less significance in creating or instigating a learning process about the product (Malik et al, 2014). In other words, advertisements have a more positive effect on consumer purchase behavior if the advertisement includes informational content (Malik et al, 2014). Added to this is the fact that, it has been discovered that the more interactive an advertisement is the more it captivates the attention of the consumer and the more impact it actually has on consumer decision (Iqbal et al, 2013).

In comparison to online advertisements, the general consensus amongst scholars about traditional methods of advertisements appears to be that there is some positive impact on consumer purchase behavior ranging from product learning, to a decrease in price sensitivity and an increase in actual purchases (Kumar and Raju, 2013). This paper argues that perhaps this is due to the fact that producers or marketing managers have more control over traditional methods of advertisements. Whereas with online advertisements, consumers are able to ignore the advertisements, pro-actively initiate the product learning process themselves thus controlling what they learn about the product which could be positive or negative.

In conclusion, we have seen the growth of technology and its impact on consumer behavior. We have looked at three ways that consumer behavior has changed, from connected consumers to changed expectations and new communication tools use. Customers now know they are powerful, what are you doing to quench their instant information thirst? When we are facing information society, the nowadays online advertisements can influence any purchase or consumption behavior on consumer purchase decisions. Furthermore, some key elements of online advertising such as word of mouth by way of online reviews on social media platforms were examined in detail as well as their impact on consumer purchase decision. Finally online advertisements in general and how they influence consumer purchase decision was also examined. From the aforementioned examination and analysis, it can be concluded that online advertisements in whatever form can have either a positive or negative impact on consumer purchase decisions. In sharp contrast, it was discovered that traditional methods of advertisements have consistent (across various studies) positive impact on consumer purchase behavior. It can also be concluded that of all the forms of online advertisement, online reviews are perhaps the most volatile and prone to resulting in a negative impact on purchase decisions. Nevertheless, it is also quite likely to bring on the most amount of sales within a short period of time. It was discovered that consumers find some online adverts annoying which also influences their decision to allow the engagement of their attention and consequently their money in making the final purchase. In addition, it was also found that there are positive correlations between online adverts and consumer purchase behavior in that the online adverts the customer's interest in a product and eventually leads to a purchase.

Reference

Afzal, S. and Rabbani Khan, J. (2015). Impact of Online and Conventional Advertisements on Consumer Buying Behavior of Branded Garments. Asian Journal of Management Sciences and Education, 4(1), pp.126 – 135.

Bakshi, G. and Gupta, S. (2013). Online Advertising and Its Impact on Consumer Buying Behavior. International Journal of Research in Finance and Marketing, 3(1), pp.21-30.

Bray, J. (2008). Consumer Behavior Theory: Approaches and Models. 1st ed. [eBook] Available at: http://eprints.bournemouth.ac.uk/10107/

Darban, A. and Li, W. (2012). The Impact of

Online Social Networks on Consumer Purchasing Decision. Masters. Jonkoping University.

Doyle, P. and Stern, P. (2006). Marketing management and strategy. 4th ed. Harlow: Pearson Education.

Jobber, D. and Ellis-Chadwick, F. (2013). Principles and Practice of Marketing. 7th ed. Berkshire: McGraw Hill Education.

Kumar, D & Raju, V. (2013). The Role of Advertising in Consumer Decision Making. IOSR Journal of Business and Management, 14(4), pp.37-45.

Li, H. and Leckenby, J. (2004). Internet Advertising Formats and Effectiveness. 1st ed. [eBook] Available at: https://brosephstalin.files.wordpress.com/2010/06/ad_format_print.pdf

Malik, M., Ghafoor, M. and Iqbal, H. (2014). The Impact of Advertisement and Consumer Perception on Consumer Buying Behaviour. International Review of Social Sciences and Humanities, 6(2), pp.55-64.

Iqbal.H., Malik, M., Ghafoor, M., Ali, Q., Hunbal, H., Noman, M. and Ahmad, B. (2013). Impact of Brand Image and Advertisements on Consumer Buying Behaviour. World Applied Sciences Journal, 23(1), pp.117 – 122.

Morrison, K. (2014). Social Media Has Changed How Consumers Shop Online [Infographic]. [Online] Adweek.com. Available at: http://www.adweek.com/socialtimes/social-media-changed-consumers-shop-online-infographic/209738

Murphy, M. (2015). Understanding consumers: How the Internet has affected purchasing habits. [Online] Blog.rdpr.co.uk. Available at: http://blog.rdpr.co.uk/how-has-the-internet-affected-purchasing-habits

Priyanka, S. (2012). A study on the impact of online advertising on consumer behaviour (with special reference to emails). International Journal of Engineering and Management Sciences, [Online] 3(4). Available at: http://scienceandnature.org/IJEMS-Vol3 (4)-Oct2012/ IJEMS_V3(4)10.pdf

Schiffman, L. and Kanuk, L. (2007). Consumer Behaviour. 9th ed. New Jersey: Prentice Hall.

Senecal, S. and Nantel, J. (2004). The influence of online product recommendations on consumers' online choices. Journal of Retailing, 80(2), pp.159-169.

Webster, Frank (2002). Theories of the Information Society. Cambridge: Routledge.

CHAPTER SIX

Factors influence technological products needs

● What does high technological product mean?

High technology, or high tech (sometimes also called frontier technology or frontier tech), is technology that is at the cutting edge: the most advanced technology available.The opposite of high tech is low technology, referring to simple, often traditional or mechanical technology; for example, a slide rule is a low-tech calculating device. Appropriate technology is a movement (and its manifestations) encompassing technological choice and application that is small-scale, affordable by locals, decentralized, labor-intensive, energy-efficient, environmentally sound, and locally autonomous. It was originally articulated as intermediate technology by the economist Ernst Friedrich "Fritz" Schumacher in his work Small Is Beautiful. Both Schumacher and many modern-day proponents of appropriate technology also emphasize the technology as people-centered.

Appropriate technology has been used to address issues in a wide range of fields. Well-known examples of appropriate technology applications include: bike- and hand-powered water pumps (and other self-powered equipment), the universal nut sheller, self-contained solar lamps and streetlights, and passive solar building designs. Today appropriate technology is often developed using open source principles, which have led to open-source appropriate technology (OSAT) and thus many of the plans of the technology can be freely found on the Internet.OSAT has been proposed as a new model of enabling innovation for sustainable development.

Appropriate technology is most commonly discussed in its relationship to economic development and as an alternative to technology transfer of more capital-intensive technology from industrialized nations to developing countries. However, appropriate technology movements can be found in both developing and developed countries. In developed countries, the appropriate technology movement grew out of the energy crisis of the 1970s and focuses mainly on environmental and sustainability issues. Today the idea is multifaceted; in some contexts, appropriate technology can be described as the simplest level of technology that can achieve the intended purpose, whereas in others, it can refer to engineering that takes adequate consideration of social and environmental ramifications. The facets are connected through robustness and sustainable living.

● Why does high technological products need to design and innovate ?
Industrial design is a process of design applied to products that are to be manufactured through techniques of mass production. Its key characteristic is that design is separated from manufacture: the creative act of determining and defining a product's form and features takes place in advance of the physical act of making a product, which consists purely of repeated, often automated, replication. This distinguishes industrial design from craft-based design, where the form of the product is determined by the product's creator at the time of its creation.

All manufactured products are the result of a design process, but the nature of this process can take many forms: it can be conducted by an individual or a large team; it can emphasize intuitive creativity or calculated scientific decision-making, and often emphasizes both at the same time; and it can be influenced by factors as varied as materials, production processes, business strategy, and prevailing social, commercial, or aesthetic attitudes. The role of an industrial designer is to create and execute design solutions for problems of form, function, usability, physical ergonomics, marketing, brand development, sustainability, and sales.

Innovation in its modern meaning is "a new idea, creative thoughts, new imaginations in form of device or method".Innovation is often also viewed as the application of better solutions that meet new requirements, unarticulated needs, or existing market needs.Such innovation takes place through the provision of more-effective products, processes, services, technologies, or business models that are made available to markets, governments and society. An innovation is something original and more effective and, as a consequence, new, that "breaks into" the market or society. Innovation is related to, but not the same as, invention,as innovation is more apt to involve the practical implementation of an invention (ie new / improved ability) to make a meaningful impact in the market or society, and not all innovations require an invention. Innovation often [quantify] manifests itself via the engineering process, when the problem being solved is of a technical or scientific nature. The opposite of innovation is exnovation. While a novel device is often described by whom? As an innovation, in economics, management science, and other fields of practice and analysis, innovation is generally considered to be the result of a process that brings together various novel ideas in such a way that they affect society. In industrial economics, innovations are created and foundby whom?Empirically from services to meet growing consumer demand.

● Why will emerging technological products need increase ?
Emerging technologies are those technical innovations that represent progressive innovations within a field for competitive advantage.
I. Emerging technological products on agriculture aspect may include:
Agricultural robot aims Research and development, trial projects ,
II. Emerging technological products on Aviation aspect may include:
Neural-sensing headset (trans-cranial neural sensing and characterization)
III. Emerging technological products on construction aspect may include:
Claytronics is an abstract future concept that combines nanoscale robotics and computer science to create individual nanometer-scale computers called claytronic atoms, or catoms, which can interact with each other to form tangible 3D objects that a user can interact with. This idea is more broadly referred to as programmable matter. Claytronics has the potential to greatly affect many areas of daily life, such as telecommunication, human-computer interfaces, and entertainment.
4-dimensional printing (4D printing; also known as 4D bioprinting, active origami, or shape-morphing systems) uses the same techniques of 3D printing through computer-programmed deposition of material in successive layers to create a three-dimensional object. However, 4D printing adds the dimension of transformation over time. It is therefore a type of programmable matter, wherein after the fabrication process, the printed product reacts with parameters within the environment (humidity, temperature, etc.,) and changes its form accordingly. The ability to do so arises from the near infinite configurations at a micrometer resolution, creating solids with engineered molecular spatial distributions and thus allowing unprecedented multifunctional performance.
A molecular assembler is a kind of molecular machine. Some biological molecules such as ribosomes fit this definition. This is because they receive

instructions from messenger RNA and then assemble specific sequences of amino acids to construct protein molecules. However, the term "molecular assembler" usually refers to theoretical human-made devices.

and

Utility fog (coined by Dr. John Storrs Hall in 1989) is a hypothetical collection of tiny robots that can replicate a physical structure.As such, it is a form of self-reconfiguring modular robotics.

All of above these Emerging technologies will be any industries' emerging need highh technological products to replace traditonal old technological products. So, their demand will be more than nowadays traditional old technological products to any industries needs. So, developed countries' industries buyers number to above these any one emerging technological products will increase in our future high technological products market.

● What is a high involvement product and characteristics of High involvement purchase to influence the brand and the kind of high technological product need?

A high involvement product is a product where extensive thought process is involved and the consumer considers a lot of variables before finally making a purchase decision. Many times, high involvement purchases involve multiple buyers or multiple influencers who influence a single buyer. An example of multiple people being involved in buying a high involvement product is when you purchase a car. If you want to purchase a car, you will surely involve your loved ones and will take review from your friends as well as on the internet. You will collect a lot of information, and then finally, once your confidence is up, you will purchase the brand you are targeting. Hence, a high involvement purchase does not involve only the buyer. It involves the public perception of the product and the brand as well.

Features of High Involvement products or High involvement purchase

High Involvement product and High involvement purchase

1) High price

The first feature of a high involvement purchase is that the price of the product is high. Because of the high price, the consumer thinks twice before the purchase. Price in itself is a subjective approach. An apartment in a good locality might be child's play for a rich person but is a dream for a poor person. Thus, for the poor, it is a very high involvement purchase. He might have to save for years before he finally decides to purchase the house. Whereas, to the rich, the purchase of such an apartment might be low involvement instead.

2) Differentiation is important

The higher the involvement in the product, the more is the differentiation required between the product or the brands. Just look at Macbook pro vs Dell XPS 13. These are 2 laptops who are at the top of their game currently. There are a lot of points differentiating them and these differentiating factors are needed. These factors create enough value to instigate the consumer in making a decision. If there is poor differentiation, then a high involvement product might lose out to a competitor who has excellent distribution. Technological innovations, product level innovations or overall features of a product can help the consumer take a faster decision in a high involvement purchase.

3) Brand recall and valuation

Influencers can be many people. It can be your son when you are buying a home theatre or an expensive mobile. It can be your friend who is driving the luxury car and recommends you to buy from the same brand. It can be your overall exposure to the brand over the years and your inclination to buy the same. It can be your family which recommends the brand, even though they have not purchased the same. In general, a brand which has a higher recall or valuation has a higher chance of winning over competitors whenever high involvement products are involved. Look at speakers of Bose which are considered as high involvement products mainly because of their premium price in a category where there are cheap speakers as well.

However, the brand valuation of bose and the performance of their speakers over the years are enough to put a consumer in awe of them. In essence, media exposure over years might instigate the consumer to keep Bose speakers as his dream home theatre system. Over a period of time, he might save money to buy those speakers and receive a superior audio experience as well as the delight of owning a premium brand.

4) Customer perceived risk

Because the price of the product is high and because the consumer has huge expectations from a high involvement product, there is a perceived risk involved in the purchase of the product. Example – A team of purchase managers decides to buy a state of the art equipment for their factory. This is a B2B high involvement purchase. Naturally, because the company is spending a huge amount for the new equipment, they have the fear that the machine should be high performing and efficient, else all the money and time invested will be wasted. Not only in B2B, even in B2C the major constraint in purchasing a high involvement product is the perceived risk factor. What if you purchase a product and it does not work as per your expectations even after investing a large amount of money? This is where branding plays a crucial role – To handle the fear of the purchase and to sooth the customer.

5) Available Information / Company communications

Another factor which is characteristic of High involvement products is the amount of information that consumers seek out about the product before the purchase. When i wanted to purchase a Macbook (a high involvement purchase because my livelihood is dependent on my laptop), i researched and researched about the differences between a Macbook and a windows laptop for months. There are sites dedicated to how Macbook works and the differences between Macbook and Windows laptops. Similarly, there are many review sites which compare televisions, high end cars, consumer appliances or anything else. These review sites give a lot of additional information of the product, which help the consumer in decision making. Not only websites, Ebrochures, printed brochures, landing pages, E-commerce pages can all help the customer in gathering information about the product. The more information the customer has, the more likely he is going to purchase the product. So it is the job of the marketing manager of an organization to ensure marketing communications is upto mark and that the users are well informed.

6) After sales service

One of the reasons that a customer might reject the idea of buying a particular high involvement product is because he comes to know from reviews that the product has very poor after sales service. You don't buy cars which don't have spare parts. A company might not buy equipment which requires too much maintenance or where after sales service is poor. The better the after sales service and customer satisfaction, the more is the likelihood of a high involvement product being sold off again and again. Hence, holistic marketing is a crucial component of high involvement purchases. A marketing organization has to present a unified front and it has to involve marketing in all aspects.

● Factors that Affect Demand for Smartphones and Tablets in the Global Market

Technological trends in 21st century have brought major changes to people's lifestyle. Technology is there everywhere from the time you wake up to the time you go to sleep and the time in between. People are using it to connect with others, to buy and sell and even to monitor their personal health and well being. Technological innovation brought several marvels including internet, social media and smart portable gadgets. While portability and convenience became important issues influencing people's choices of the kind of products and technology they choose to use, smart-phones grew in demand because of the large range of applications (apps) they offered. People are now accessing the internet and using it for longer in their day to day lives. Social media has also altered the way we connect with people and given arise to a new need to stay connected on the go. People like to remain online around the clock even when they are asleep and have all the information they need on their fingertips. Nothing serves this purpose better than a smart-phone or a tablet and this is the main reason behind the popularity of these smarter gadgets which despite being smaller than laptops can serve several uses for which a person would earlier need a computer or a laptop. These smart-phones come loaded with so many functions and cater to our several needs. In this article, we will discuss what factors can influence their demand and how their popularity is affected by ongoing technological changes.

Portable technology is there everywhere in our lives from smaller laptops to large screen smart-phones, tablets and wearable technology. One main reason that has led to the growth in demand and use of portable technology is the changing lifestyle of people in the 21st century. It is a busier world where every second counts and people want to remain active and productive at their best. Smart-phones and laptops do not just help you stay connected but also come loaded with productivity tools. A basic email and social media are compulsory functions that every smart phone has. However, there are other apps and tools too that have made it simpler for people to stay active via the internet even when commuting. The most basic purpose that a smart phone serves is to keep you connected with your near and dear ones. However, there is much more. People also need their daily dose of entertainment whenever they need it during the day. These smart phones can provide you access to streaming videos, music, and create your own videos and shoot images. It caters to people's productivity as well as leisure needs. If you have a smart-phone with you, you do not have a chance to grow bored because you have just so many options from watching videos to video calling your friends and playing video games. So, the utility and convenience offered by the smart-phones and tablets is the reason that their demand has grown. Smart-phones are smaller in size than tablets but several of them come with large screen sizes of 6 inches or more which is sufficient to play videos without needing more quality and clarity. However, a large number of users like to use tablets for reading e-books and for playing streaming videos. Amazon's kindle offers thousands of e-books which can be accessed through a single account. You cannot have the same convenience when you use a laptop because you cannot carry it around with as much ease as a smart-phone or laptop which you can carry in a small bag or even your pocket. Amid their changing lifestyles, people demand extra convenience and utility because they are now more busy and productive than ever. A very large and growing crowd of professionals cannot do without a smart-phone or a tablet because it has to send and receive emails or even other files and it can be the situation of an emergency any time anywhere. The need for higher productivity has given rise to new needs which can be catered to through smarter gadgets that are easier to carry around and use. Most young people have the Amazon app on their phones and like to shop at a tap for their small and big needs.

Changing demographics of the global population have also affected the demand for smart-phones and tablets. During the recent decade, the demographic composition of the global population has changed a lot. Baby boomers have moved out of the global workforce in large numbers and millenials joined it. The millenials were born with technology. They are more tech savvy than the previous generation and spend more time using technology and internet. The millenials including the teenagers use more technological devices and internet is an essential part of their lives. They were born in the era of email and constitute the largest population on social media. Facebook, Twitter and YouTube are their favorite social media stops and they cannot do without spending sometime on each of them daily. Their needs are different from the previous generations and not just social media and social connection, they do much more online and using smart-phones and tablets. The millenials or the youth constitute the largest segment of smart-phone and tablet consumers and several of the own more than one. These people spend their leisure time differently than the baby boomers and are more likely to shop online. These millenials use their smart-phones for so many purposes including email, surfing the web, for entertainment, shopping and several other odd jobs including professional uses. They also like reading e-books and blogs on their tablets. In this way, the changing demographics of the world population and the increased use of internet technology have added to the demand for smart-phones and tablets. Another important reason that the use of smart-phones among youth has kept growing is because they use it for taking selfies and keep posting them on Facebook and other social media channels. Sometimes the love for smart-phones also takes the form of an addiction. Some years ago texting had become a bane for parents because their kids remained busy texting their friends on their phones. It had taken the form of an addiction. With the arrival of the smartphone, new channels of communication like WhatsApp and video calling are available which still keep the young people and teenagers engaged on their smart-phone screen. In a youth's life, a smart-phone plays several roles helping him save important files, pictures and staying connected with his dear friends as well as passing time when he is alone. In US, the number of smart-phone users is highest in the 18- 49 age group. (Source: Statista)

Apart from technological and demographic factors, there are some more that have held to the growing demand of smart-phones and tablets. Economic factors have also aided the growth and proliferation of smart-phone technology. The world economy is back on track since after the recession and globally the level of employment has also risen. With returning economic activity, people have more disposable income to spend on the technology and lifestyle products. Smart-Phones and tablets are not just technological gadgets but an inseparable part of a modern and fast moving lifestyle. In this decade the middle class population around the globe has seen a major rise in its income level. People have more extra income to spend on technological products and online shopping. There are several brands in the market which cater to a large group of consumers from the low end to the high end segment. High end smart-phones made by Apple or Samsung have increased in demand because of their excellent quality and functions. Moreover, people are now having better and easier access to finance for their purchases. Credit cards and easy EMIs have also somewhere helped churn demand for lifestyle and technology products. More people are buying smart-phones and tablets using their credit cards and on EMIs. So, the role of economic factors is important with regards to the demand for smart gadgets like smart-phones and tablets. The sales of these products are particularly high in the developed and developing economies and which again proves the importance of economic factors. In nations where people's purchasing power is higher, the sales of these gadgets are also high. As per a Statista report, the number of smart-phone users is highest in three countries including India, China and US followed by Brazil, Russia, Japan and Germany.

Apart from all these factors there are social factors that also influence the demand for smart-phones. Social influences also play an important role in churning demand for these products. For a very large number of smart-phone owners, it is not just a cool gadget but a lifestyle and status symbol. Several of them purchase these products after seeing a close friend or dear one using it. Many own them just because they want to stay connected with their friends or because their friend bought a new one. The degree of exposure to technology in a society or culture also affects the demand for smart-phones and tablets there. In the western nations and the developed and fast developing nations of Asia, the demand for smart-phones is higher because kids are exposed to technology at an early age there. In the nations where the level of technological growth is higher, the demand for smart-phones is correspondingly higher. Globalization brought several changes that made people adopt modern lifestyles. As their lifestyles grew more modern, these gadgets became an intrinsic part of their lifestyles. Some more factors that can also lead to higher demand are the brand name, brand equity, level of investment in marketing and overall popularity. The popularity of Apple products in the high end market is higher because of their quality and extraordinary technology. Samsung and other brands invest heavily in marketing of their smartphones. Its pricing strategy also affects demand. A competitive pricing strategy helps create extra demand for a product. In this way, you can see there are several factors that affect the demand for smart-phones and tablets in the global market. Technological, economic and lifestyle factors are of special importance with regards to understanding why people buy and use smart-phones. As per reports the use of these smart gadgets will continue to grow in the coming years.

On conclusion, factors Influence Industrial Productive industry raises high technological manufacturing products needs. Some of the important factors influencing industrial productivity are : (i) Technological Development (ii) Quality of Human Resources (iii) Availability of Finance (iv) Managerial Talent (v) Government Policy (vi) Natural Factors.

However, the factors affecting industrial productivity are inter-related and interdependent and it is a difficult task to evaluate the influence of each individual factor on the overall productivity of industrial units.

The impact of certain important factors is briefly examined below:

(i) Technological Development:

Technological development plays an important part to influence the industrial productivity. "The application of motive power and mechanical improvements to the process of production has accelerated the peace of industrialisation to an unprecedented degree, and has given us the vision of the vast and unexplored frontiers that still lie ahead of us in the realm of applied science and technology."

The technological factors include degree of mechanisation, technical know-how, product design, etc. Improvement in any of the technological factors will contribute towards the increase in industrial productivity. In India, application of mechanical power, introduction of semi-automatic and automatic machines, improvements in the production processes, better Morale and Productivity integration of production processes and higher degree of specialisation have contributed a lot towards the increases in industrial productivity.

(ii) Quality of Human Resources:

Manpower plays a significant role. In raising industrial productivity in most of the industries. If the labour force is not adequately qualified and/or is not properly motivated, all the steps taken to increase the industrial productivity will have no result the employees' performance and attitudes have an immense effect on the productivity of any industrial unit. Three important factors which influence the productivity of labour area (a) ability of the worker, (b) willingness of the worker, and (c) the environment under which he has to work.

(iii) Availability of Finance:

The ambitious plans of an industrial unit to increase the productivity will remain mere dreams if adequate financial resources are not available to introduce technical improvements and give appropriate training to the workers. The greater the degree of mechanistion to be introduced, the greater is the need for capital. Capital will also be required for investment in research and development activities, advertisement campaign, better working conditions to the workers, up-keep of plant and machinery, etc.

(iv) Managerial Talent:

The significance of managerial talent has increased with the advancement in technology. Professional managers are required to make better use of the new technological development. Since the modern enterprises are run on a large scale, the managers must possess imagination, judgment and willingness to take imitative. The managers should be devoted towards their profession and they should understand their social responsibilities towards the owners of the business, workers, customers, suppliers. Government, and the society this is essential if the managers want to manage their organisations effectively. The managers should have conceptual, human relations and technical skills in order to increases the productivity of the enterprise.

(v) Government Policy:

The industrial policies of the Government have an important impact on the industrial productivity; The Government should frame and implement such policies which create favourable conditions for saving, investment, flow of capital from one industrial sector to another and conservation of national resources. Certain industries may be granted protection, and incentives may be given to the others for the development in view of the national interest. The Government should flow the taxation policy which does not discourage the further expansion of business

(vi) Natural Factors:

The natural factors such as physical, geographical and climatic exercise considerable impact on the industrial productivity. The relative importance of these factors depends upon the nature of the industry, goods and services produced and the extent to which physical conditions are controlled. "The geological and physical factors play a very dominant role in determining the productivity of extractive industries likes coal-mining in which the physical output per head is greatly influenced by the depth of the coal-mines, the thickness of the coal seams, the topography of the region and the quality of coal available. In other industries like tailoring, grain-milling, hosiery, soap-making, confectionary, medium and coarse cotton manufacturing, etc., the geographical, geological and physical factors exercise little influence on productivity".

● FACTORS THAT INFLUENCE HIGH TECHNOLOGICAL PRODUCT DEVELOPMENT NEED

Product Analysis is the process of identifying, looking at or disassembling a product and identifying its main features. The aim is to understand more about a product and improve it in the future. Many factors influence the development of a product, some are listed below.

The rich picture above gives an outline to some of the many factors that affect the development of a product. Below is more detail regarding each of the points mentioned above.

● COST

The cost of the materials and labour required to manufacture the product.

The price potential customers are prepared to pay for the product.

● ERGONOMICS
The product may be designed for human use. As a result ergonomics (sizes etc...) will pay a major role. Click here for more detail about ergonomics.

● MATERIALS
The availability of materials and the development of new, hi-technology materials will have an influence on the final design of a product.

● CUSTOMER REQUIREMENTS
The customer will have great influence over the way a product is designed and develops. As a product is designed it is normal for potential customers to be questioned about the type of product or design that they prefer. For example, when designing a mobile phone a design team will show potential customers several designs and make changes according to their likes and dislikes.

● INDUSTRIAL PRODUCTION
All products are manufactured through one of the following manufacturing techniques:
Single Item / Prototype / One Off
Batch Production
Continuous Production
Just in Time
When designing a product the most desirable production technique may influence the way the final product looks.

● COMPANY IDENTITY
The product may have to display the company image. Most companies are proud of their public image. This may determine the colour scheme applied to the product, the way it looks or even the materials that are used in its manufacture (i.e. recycled materials).

● AESTHETICS
The shape and form of the product may determine the layout of circuits or mechanisms etc.. inside it. Products are often designed to look stylish. The style applied to the outside of a product can quite easily influence the technology inside it. Aesthetics can also alter the production /

manufacturing techniques through which it is made.

● FASHION

The fashion of the time influences the design of products. Usually people want to buy up to date items not ones based on 'last years look'.

● CULTURE

Some products are aimed at different cultures and countries. A product acceptable in one culture may be looked up one as offensive or less desirable in another. The use of colours and colour schemes are a good example of this. Click here for further details.

● FUNCTIONS

The number of functions a product has to perform will inevitably affect its design. Exactly what is the product going to do?

● ENVIRONMENT

Many people (potential customers) are concerned about their environment and the damage to it caused by industrial production. When designing a product it may be wise to ensure that the materials can be recycled or the product itself can be manufactured from a large proportion of recycled material.

On conclusion, all of these factors will influence any kinds of high technological products need in market.